**Custom
Combining
on the
Great
Plains**

CUSTOM COMBINING ON THE GREAT PLAINS

A History

By Thomas D. Isern

University of Oklahoma Press: Norman

Library of Congress Cataloging in Publication Data

Isern, Thomas D. (Thomas Dean), 1952–
   Custom combining on the Great Plains.

   Bibliography: p.
   Includes index.
   1. Combines (Agricultural machinery)—Great Plains—
History.   2. Wheat—Great Plains—Harvesting—History.
I. Title.
S699.I78   338.1′73115′0978   81-2781
                                    AACR2

Copyright © 1981 by the University of Oklahoma Press, Norman,
Publishing Division of the University of Oklahoma.
Manufactured in the U.S.A.
First edition.

To my parents,
Orville and Marie Isern,
wheat farmers

Contents

Illustrations

ix

FIGURES

Tables

Preface

To farmers on the Great Plains, custom combining is an accepted institution, one so taken for granted that its origins are obscure. This history refreshes the memory of those beginnings and traces the development of the business to the present.

The subjects of the study are known variously as "custom combiners," "custom harvesters," "contract harvesters," and even "wheaties," but most often as "custom cutters." Owners of combines may do custom work locally, but I focus here on itinerant custom cutters who travel with the harvest. The geographic scope is the Great Plains of the United States, with some attention to parallel developments in the prairie provinces of Canada. My perspective is frankly environmental, and I interpret custom combining as one of many peculiar adaptations that characterize life on the Great Plains. This is not the only way to view custom combining, but it is a useful way. Research for this study has been tipped somewhat toward the southern plains at the expense of the northern plains because of my own location during its preparation. Custom cutting, however, is more characteristic of the southern plains than of the northern plains, and so the bias is not indefensible.

I have made certain decisions in regard to documentation that should be explained. Where the text runs for pages without a footnote, it usually means that my statements are based on personal observation of custom cutters and on informal conversations with them in such places as grain elevators and taverns, contacts too loose to be termed "interviews." This is especially true in the chapter entitled "A Peculiar Style of Life." I could have cited my field notes, but that seemed pompous.

This work should be regarded as exploratory. Economists, geographers, and sociologists may launch specialized and structured investigations of their own. I have carried the inquiry far enough to draw some significant generalizations.

Thanks beyond words are due a number of members of the Department of History, Oklahoma State University, especially Dr. Norbert Mahnken and Dr. LeRoy Fischer, for their help and encouragement. The entire staff of the Edmund Lowe Library at Oklahoma State was tireless in searching out even the most obscure sources for me, but I must single out the efforts of Vicki Phillips, John Phillips, and Terry Bassford. Finally, I have been amazed and gratified by the courtesy and assistance of the many custom cutters I have interviewed. I garnered not only their recollections but also quite a few free meals.

Even as I compose this preface, the men and women who follow the harvest remain a source of fascination for me. Although I grew up on a wheat farm in Kansas and always was familiar with the business of custom cutting, I never made the harvest with a custom outfit. I had friends who did it, but I always stayed home to plow while they trekked on north to such magic places as Devil's Lake, North Dakota, or Cutbank, Montana. Field work for this study helped me learn the facts and the folkways of the harvest through observation.

I especially recall an evening in June, 1977, that I spent in the North Canadian River valley west of Taloga, Oklahoma. This is a region of rugged gypsum hills covered with gypweed and buffalo grass, but the river valley itself supports fine farms. I had spent the day photographing and talking to custom cutters. At nightfall I was sitting in the yard of a farmstead perched on the divide north of the river. I could see four or five miles across the valley to the divide on the other side and six or seven miles up and down the river. As darkness fell, lights popped on one by one all over the valley.

Some moved in great circles, following each other around, while others moved in straight lines and sped away, soon to return. The valley seemed inhabited by a great swarm of fireflies, except that out of it rose a deep, pulsating rumble, not so much a loud sound as an overwhelming one. The distant clamor of hundreds of machines went unnoticed during the day, but with the darkness it filled every gulch and gulley. At that lonely moment I understood something of the hold that the harvest has on the people who follow it.

Custom
Combining
on the
Great
Plains

William F. Dunekack operated this binder in Barton County, Kansas, at the turn of the century, but later relied on the header to harvest his wheat.
Photo courtesy of Norma Briel.

Chapter 1
Harvester's Heritage
The Background

Custom cutters seldom are introspective. Year by year they follow the yellow road of the wheat belt north, giving little thought to the circumstances that brought their occupation into being. Yet the same conditions still affect their lives, dictating practices for them and for the farmers on whom their business depends.

Residents of the Great Plains who are engaged in agriculture or in related pursuits, such as contract harvesting, are buffeted by forces both environmental and economic that are often contradictory and always beyond control. They do not create their geographic environment, but adapt to their surroundings. Neither can any individual alter the national agricultural economy, for farming is such a competitive and individualistic industry that no one operator can affect the market.

The development of wheat farming on the plains showed the interplay of these forces. Wheat became the staple because it was suited to the area. Farmers on the southern plains needed a crop that would make use of spring rains, mature early, and be in the bin before the hottest days of summer arrived. After attempts to grow corn, in the 1870s settlers in Kansas turned to soft winter wheat and during the next decade to hard red winter wheat.[1] Farmers on the northern plains required a crop that would flourish with a short growing season and limited rainfall. Their answer was spring wheat—first soft spring wheat carried from the prairies to the east, then the better-adapted hard spring wheat.

3

Improvements in wheat varieties and farming practices enabled farmers to push the wheat frontier west on the high plains of the United States and north and west into the prairie provinces of Canada. Methods of tillage evolved from the dust mulch espoused by proponents of dry farming at the turn of the century to the protective stubble retained by practitioners of no-till farming in the 1970s. The transition from horses to steam engines to gasoline tractors allowed ordinary family farmers to overcome problems of scale that had hampered even the most efficient of the bonanza farmers of the nineteenth century.

Although such improvements in technology made the expansion of wheat farming feasible, it was weather and the agricultural economy that determined when farmers extended or retracted the wheat frontier. Drought and depression ended the agricultural boom of the 1880s, but soaring prices for grain during World War I brought a new wave of sodbusting that spilled onto the high plains. With increased mechanization the plow-up continued, despite hard times in the 1920s, and contributed to the disastrous dust storms of the 1930s. The relentless cycle recurred twice more: farmers broke new ground when World War II brought high prices, and they suffered blowouts in the early 1950s; when prices spurted upward due to exports in the early 1970s fencerow-to-fencerow planting brought dust storms back once more. Worse yet, along with each reversal in the weather came a collapse in the market for wheat. Thus, although technological improvements for farming on the plains were continual, they were implemented in a series of surges.

This trend also was evident in particular aspects of wheat farming on the plains, such as harvesting and threshing. Changes in techniques of harvesting and threshing followed two general paths. Methods became more mechanized and capital-intensive, decreasing the need for unskilled laborers, as was the case with almost all commercial farming in the United States. In addition other innovations met the peculiar needs of farmers on the plains. Both types of modifications, those of mechanization and those of adaptation, received their impetus from the same cycles of boom and bust that affected wheat farming as a whole.

In any area of the Great Plains before the development of transportation to markets for grain, harvesting went through a pioneer stage of improvisation. Settlers used whatever rude means they could to gather a small crop for local use. On the eastern fringe of the plains they often relied on the scythe and cradle to garner grain. Behind the blade of the scythe, swung rhythmically from stooped shoulders, several thin fingers of wood caught the falling stalks. The cradler left the grain in piles, and a second man followed behind to tie the piles into bundles. Even on the high plains, in areas broken during the early twentieth century methods of harvesting were primitive at first. Some pioneers in the Texas Panhandle tied a cowhide behind a wheel-driven mowing machine to catch the falling grain and then left the grain in mounds to be tied into bundles or handled loose.[2]

Such methods gave way to more sophisticated ones as soon as farmers gained access to markets. By the time settlement moved onto the plains in the 1870s, techniques of harvesting had become standardized in the Midwest. Farmers harvested small grains with a binder, a horse-drawn implement with a sickle like that of a mowing machine and a revolving reel to sweep the grain across the sickle. The cut grain fell on a platform or table with a revolving canvas belt. The belt carried the grain to the side and elevated it to a mechanical knotter, which tied the grain into bundles. These were dropped in the stubble behind the binder, and shockers, or stookers, followed behind to shock them. The farmer either allowed his grain to stand in the shock until time for threshing or hauled it to a central location to be stacked.[3]

This system worked well over most of North Dakota, South Dakota, and western Canada, as well as in the eastern portions of the central and southern plains. In other parts of the plains it broke down under environmental pressures. As early as the 1870s farmers in central Kansas discovered that in years of little rainfall the wheat straw was so short that binders failed to tie good bundles.[4] Harvesting with a binder also re-

This header outfit worked on the farm of Albert Peter, Sr. (standing on ground in front of stack), in Barton County, Kansas, about 1910. *Photo courtesy of Rollie Peter.*

quired the seasonal services of numerous horses and men—binder drivers, bundle-wagon drivers, shockers, and stackers. Farmers therefore adopted the header, which tied no bundles and could be operated with less hand labor.

The header was a wonderfully simple machine. It had a sickle, a reel, and a table like those of a binder, only wider. The sickle snipped the wheat stalks close to the head, and the loose heads moved up a chute by means of a canvas conveyer

belt and dropped into the bed of a wagon moving alongside. Because the header was wider and heavier than the binder, it could not be pulled to the side of the drawbar, but was pushed from behind by a team of horses or mules in traces. The header eliminated the need for shockers, because the wagon drivers hauled the grain directly to stacks. Economies of scale favored the header over the binder in areas of large acreages like the Great Plains. The header supplanted the

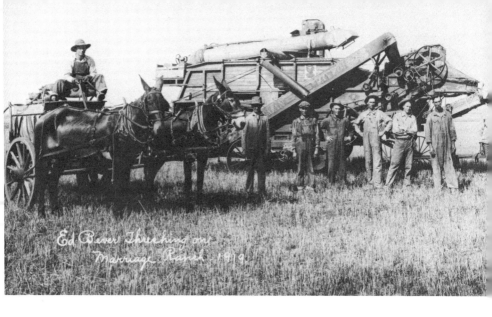

Ed Beaver Threshing on
Marriage Ranch 1919

binder over most of the southern and central plains, as well as
in western Montana and in some of the western parts of the
Dakotas.[5]

The binder held its own against the header in most parts of
the Dakotas and in Canada because of differences between
winter wheat and spring wheat. Winter wheat ripened evenly. Farmers entered the fields with headers shortly before the
wheat became dead ripe, confident that there would be no
grain in the field so green that it might cause their stacks to
heat and spoil. Spring wheat ripened unevenly and, if not
allowed to dry in the shock, spoiled in the stack. Thus the
farmers who were forced to rely on the binder consoled themselves with the knowledge that they were able to begin harvesting grain at a greener stage than those using the header.[6]

Like harvesting, threshing on the plains also went through
an isolated, primitive stage at first. Some farmers separated

Ed Bever (standing by engine wheel) owned this
custom threshing outfit on the Marriage Ranch near
Mullinville, Kansas, in 1919. His son, Alpha "Hap"
Bever, would become a custom combiner.
Photo courtesy of Flava Bever.

the grain from the straw by beating it with a flail (a staff with a
bar attached by a thong) and then throwing the grain into the
air to let the wind drive out the chaff. Others used horses or
oxen to tread out the grain. Stationary threshing machines
provided the capacity needed by commercial farmers on the
plains once they had access to markets. Until the 1890s these
generally were powered by draft animals walking in circles to
turn drive shafts. Thereafter, steam engines furnished power
to drive larger separators.[7]

Methods of threshing on the plains, like those of harvesting, settled into patterns unlike those farther east. In the
Midwest the practice of cooperative threshing came into its
own in the early twentieth century. In a neighborhood either
some local farmer owned an engine and a separator or a group
of men pooled their resources and purchased machinery
jointly. Each summer the farmers turned out to thresh each

other's grain, trading labor and getting full use from the single threshing outfit, proceeding with the work according to the bylaws of their threshing cooperative.[8]

On the Great Plains cooperative threshing gained few footholds. Instead, it became the practice for some aspiring capitalist in each locality to buy an engine and a separator, which were generally larger than those used in the Midwest. The independent thresherman assembled a crew of workers and offered his whole outfit, machinery and labor, to farmers for custom threshing of the grain that they had harvested. The thresherman charged for work by the number of bushels threshed. Farmers on the plains found custom threshing suited their needs. The extensive nature of wheat farming there meant that they needed large threshing capacity, but they were hesitant or unable to invest the amount of money necessary to buy a large separator and a powerful engine. The thresherman provided machinery at a reasonable cost and only when it was needed. He furnished expertise in the persons of his engineer and separator man, individuals skilled in handling the machines that they prized; and he relieved the farmer of the responsibility for recruiting the numerous laborers required for threshing. Custom threshing reached its peak during World War I and the early 1920s.[9] The great steam engines were emblems of mechanical prowess. The panorama of a summer's morning in the wheatlands was enough to convince anyone of the distinctive nature of agriculture there: fields of stubble stretched in all directions with stacks of headed wheat grouped here and there like loaves on a table, or else shocks of bound grain standing in precise lines; the smell of burning coal or straw was in the air; columns of smoke rose from engines building pressure; and steaming whistles summoned laborers to the stacks.

The creation of such rustic scenes depended on migratory labor. Intensive demand for transient labor developed at successive points from south to north as the summer's harvesting and threshing progressed. The workers who met the demand came mostly from the states of the Mississippi River Valley. Farmers made the harvest in hopes of supplementing their income in poor years, urban workers gambled on the chance of making high wages for a few months, and students hoped to earn enough money to support another year's schooling. In the early 1920s perhaps 100,000 men made the harvest. The United States Employment Service assumed the task of recruiting workers and directing them where they were needed, as did the Canadian Department of Labor. No one bindlestiff worked his way all the way from Texas to Canada, but most moved from south to north for some distance. The workers sought to travel as little as possible by first aiding some farmer in the harvest and then joining a threshing crew to work in the same area for the rest of the summer. Most threshermen moved their outfits only short distances, within their own localities, although an occasional entrepreneur might first thresh in the winter wheat region and then ship his machinery north by rail for a second season in the spring wheat region. Nearly all laborers, however, found it necessary to travel with the harvest in order to stay at work.[10]

The coming of the combined harvester, or combine, suspended prevailing traditions of the harvest. The rapid adoption of the new machine on the plains again exemplified the evolution of distinctive practices of harvesting in the area. An invention developed in other parts of the country was adapted to fit the needs of farmers on the plains, and then it was implemented at a time when economic conditions demanded it.

The inventors of the first working combined harvester were Hiram Moore and John Hascall of Kalamazoo County, Michigan. After the inventors tested their machine in the late 1830s, Andrew and Abner Moore (no relation to Hiram Moore) operated combines built according to the original design in Michigan at least until 1853. These men were the first custom combiners, cutting wheat for various farmers in the area. The early combines in Michigan threshed well, saved labor, and proved economical. They incorporated most of the mechanical principles basic to later combines. A reciprocating sickle cut the stalks, a toothed reel pushed the grain onto the platform, and a canvas apron delivered it to a threshing cylinder.

11

Screens and a fan cleaned the grain. The combine's header, twelve feet wide, extended to the right of the machine. Eight pairs of horses supplied power for the combine, for its moving parts were driven from a ground wheel. A driver walked beside each pair of horses. A wagon drawn alongside received the sacks of grain threshed.

Although competition from the inexpensive reaper prevented the general adoption of the combine in Michigan, an unusual sequence of events established it in California, where expansive wheat ranches offered golden wealth to rival that of the mines. In 1854, Andrew Moore and a partner named George Leland shipped a combine around Cape Horn to California. Leland that year combined about 600 acres for wheat ranchers on a custom arrangement, but his clients failed to pay him for the work. After a year prospecting for gold, Leland sold the combine in 1856. His son then operated the machine for the new owner, but when he neglected to grease the joints properly, heat from friction ignited a fire that destroyed the combine.[11]

After this false start the combine took root in the Golden State. Local mechanics and farmers had been impressed enough with the machine operated by Leland that by the late 1850s they had constructed more combines along similar lines. By the early 1860s the Monitor combines built by John Horner of Alameda County were impressive enough that local harvest workers, fearful of mechanical competition, set fire to one of the combines in the field.

More wheat ranchers in California constructed combines for their own use, and during the 1880s commercial production began. Combines built by Daniel Best, Benjamin Holt, and other manufacturers replaced headers in California in the 1890s, and after 1900 they rolled into the hilly wheatlands of Washington's Palouse Valley. These combines of the far West were cumbersome, but effective. Their headers were as wide as twenty feet. Thirty-two or more horses pulled each machine, with the driver perched on a tiny chair overhanging the teams. A man sat on a platform on the side of the combine to sew bags of grain shut and drop them in the stubble.[12]

Only a few of these monsters appeared east of the Rocky Mountains before World War I. As early as 1901 a sixteen-foot Best combine was used west of Great Bend, Kansas, by F. Neeland Thomas. He celebrated July 4 with a field-to-mouth demonstration, cutting a couple of bushels of wheat and sending it to a local mill. There it was ground into flour and baked into loaves, which went on sale in the evening of the same day. Several other combines harvested in the same region in the next few years, but the time for widespread adoption of the combine there had not yet arrived. Large as wheat farms were in western Kansas, they did not compare with the wheat ranches of California. Moreover, frequent crop failures on the plains made investment in huge combines impractical.[13]

Early, isolated introductions of the combine also took place in Saskatchewan and Montana. A man named Edmunds and another named E. J. C. Shand brought a Holt combine to Spy Hill, Saskatchewan, from California in 1910. They pulled the twenty-foot machine with a tractor. For four years they combined about 600 acres of wheat or flax annually, but they quit farming and abandoned the combine in 1914. Although they pronounced the combine a success, few paid heed. Curtis Baldwin, later to become vice-president of Gleaner-Baldwin Corporation, experimented with a homemade combine on his farm near Aneroid, Saskatchewan, from 1913 to 1919. In Montana it was reported that several combines from California were used in 1910 and after, but with little publicizing of the results.[14]

Two conditions were lacking for the combine to make its home on the plains. First, some economic jolt was required to force farmers to abandon the headers, binders, threshers, and bindlestiffs to which they were accustomed. Next, the ungainly combine had to undergo adaptation according to the specific needs of farmers on the plains.

World War I provided the economic stimulus. Rising prices for grain brought advancement of the wheat frontier. Conscription and defense work absorbed many of the seasonal laborers required by farmers. Fewer hands were available to

13

harvest more acres, and so, in 1917 and 1918, farmers on the southern plains purchased combines, reluctantly at first. The combines they chose were known as prairie models, with headers ranging from twelve to sixteen feet. They filled the need for swift harvesting with limited labor, but were not so large and expensive that the investment was prohibitive in that time of prosperity. Prairie combines were pulled by either horses or tractors, and they bore auxiliary engines to replace ground wheels in driving the threshing parts.[15]

Sales of combines increased rapidly after World War I. This was part of the general trend toward mechanization in wheat farming at the time. Although hard times came in 1921, farmers already had seen the benefits of the new machines. Kansas, with more winter wheat than any other state, also had the most combines. Farmers there purchased about 1,500 combines in 1919 and 1920. By 1926, according to the Kansas State Board of Agriculture, 8,274 combines were in use in the state and harvested more than 30 percent of the acreage in wheat. By 1930, 27,000 of the 75,000 combines in the United States were in Kansas. Some of these machines were combines with headers eight feet or less in width, designed to be driven by the power takeoff of a tractor and to be used in the Midwest. Farmers with limited capital and acreage used these smaller combines, which came on the market in 1926.[16]

Other states of the southern plains adopted the combine at about the same time. Seven combines harvested in northwest Texas in 1919; by 1927, 2,682 were reported there. Comparable figures were unavailable for Oklahoma, but in 1926 researchers at the state experiment station considered use of the combine in the state "past the experimental stage" and "the most economical method of harvesting wheat when conditions are favorable for its use."[17]

In 1926 the combine's impact was such that the United States Department of Agriculture made a survey of its use on the southern plains and in the Judith Basin of Montana. This important study, published in 1928 as *The Combined Harvester-Thresher in the Great Plains*, amounted to an official blessing for the combine. The study focused on five counties, one each in Texas, Oklahoma, Kansas, Nebraska, and Montana. The survey clearly showed the types of combines gaining acceptance on the plains. Machines with headers of sixteen feet made up nearly 40 percent of the sample of 268 combines found, with twelve- and fifteen-foot sizes also popular. Many of the machines had come equipped with a smaller header and had been fitted with extensions to widen the swath. At that time nearly all the combines were drawn by tractors. The cost of a prairie combine was between $2,000 and $3,000, but a power takeoff model might be bought for as little as $1,000. Most of the combines in use had been purchased within the past two years.

Operators of combines harvested mostly wheat, but also had success with other crops, especially grain sorghum, or milo. The popular sixteen-foot model was found to harvest an average of 682 acres in a year. An acre of wheat that required 2.8 man-hours to harvest and thresh with a header and a stationary thresher could be gleaned in only .75 man-hours with a combine. Grain losses were less with the combine, as was the total cost of harvesting and threshing.[18]

Despite the approval of the Department of Agriculture, the combine gained acceptance on the southern plains only by overcoming initial objections and problems. Because wheat had to be dead ripe before it could be cut with the combine, use of the machine delayed the beginning of harvest, increasing the likelihood that a hailstorm might level the crop. Farmers found that they could not hurry their wheat, but had to wait until it had dried to a moisture content of about 15 percent; otherwise it would spoil in the bin. In wet years weeds in the fields caused problems, because seeds and stalks of weeds in the grain increased the moisture content. Storage in elevators and on the farm had to be handled more efficiently, because, while threshing had gone on all summer with stationary separators, all the wheat was threshed during a short harvest period with combines and required storage immediately. Millers at first were prejudiced against wheat har-

Southern plains farmers like George Sturn (on combine) and
Alfred Sturn (on tractor), pictured near Bushton in July, 1929,
eagerly adopted the combine.
Photo courtesy of Joe Habiger.

vested with a combine and graded it down. The relative un-
importance of these problems, however, was expressed best
by L. C. Aicher of the agricultural experiment station at Fort
Hays, Kansas, when he said, "It isn't the fault of the combine
so much as the fact that we are inexperienced in the handling
of the combine."[19]

Conditions on the northern plains were somewhat different,
but Montana provided the combine a path of entry into the
area. In 1917 the Montana Farming Corporation near Hardin,
soon to become the famous Campbell Farming Corporation,
bought four combines, but at the end of World War I there
probably were not fifty combines in Montana. Although a few
farmers bought combines each year thereafter, still only 144
were sold in 1925. Sales increased rapidly in the next few
years, as the combine entered every part of the state where
wheat was grown, and 1,685 were sold in 1928. The combine
succeeded in the winter wheat region of Montana for the
same reasons it had farther south, and to an even greater de-

16

gree: farms were larger and workers fewer. Moreover, farmers raising both winter wheat and spring wheat could extend the use of their machines over two harvests.[20]

Spring wheat farmers in the Dakotas delayed in adopting the combine for much the same reasons they had preferred the binder over the header. Their spring wheat ripened unevenly, was plagued by weeds, and often had a rank growth of straw. If a farmer postponed harvesting until all the grain in a field was ripe enough for combining, then the weeds flourished and the grain lodged. In addition, the farms of the Dakotas were smaller than those of Montana.[21]

Manufacturers responded to the complaints of farmers and researchers in the spring wheat region by offering the windrow harvester in 1927. In 1926 managers of the Campbell Farming Corporation in Montana had improvised windrowers by hitching binders in staggered formation with the tying mechanisms removed and with extension elevators delivering the cut grain to a single windrow. They had threshed the windrows using Holt combines with the headers removed and with hay loaders lifting the grain into the threshers. Some of the first windrowers offered for general sale in 1927 discharged the cut grain at the end of the platform, others at the middle. Most were powered from a ground wheel, although after a few years models connected to the tractor power takeoff were more common. Soon manufacturers added pans from which the grain slid gently onto the stubble, so that it would not fall through to the ground. Suspended a few inches from the ground, the grain dried until it was picked up by a combine fitted with a pickup header, a header that, instead of a sickle, had wire teeth that lifted the grain onto the platform.

Windrowing reduced shattering, farmers believed; it also allowed both wheat and weeds to dry uniformly in the windrow. The windrower was the machine for impatient farmers who could not stand to watch while neighbors started their binders. Windrowers could enter the field just a couple of days later than binders, and combines could begin picking up windrows before grain in the shock was ready for threshing.

17

The only problems were the increased expense of windrowing and the possibility that heavy rains might drive windrows to ground.[22]

The windrower prompted introduction of the combine in the Dakotas, although the binder remained in use for several decades. In 1927 there were only about 180 combines in South Dakota and 200 in North Dakota. The next year the figures were 648 for South Dakota and 1,172 for North Dakota. Combines generally were smaller in the Dakotas than in the winter wheat regions. About two out of five were power take-off models, the rest prairie models, with the power takeoff machines more prevalent in the eastern parts of the states.[23]

Combines won their way into the spring wheat regions of western Canada at about the same time as in the Dakotas. In 1922, Massey-Harris Company placed a twelve-foot combine on the Dominion Experimental Farm at Swift Current, Saskatchewan, while International Harvester Corporation placed one at the experimental farm at Cabri. Although generally it was thought that the short harvesting season would make combines impractical in the prairie provinces, they performed admirably in trials during the next six years. Officials of the experimental station in Saskatchewan aided in establishing the combine in the region by publicizing the favorable results of their tests, findings that were supported by farmers trying the machine at the same time.

Early users of combines in western Canada, who bought them despite warnings, even from implement dealers, of the unsuitability of the machines, practiced straight cutting of their wheat with great success. The number of combines in western Canada swelled from just four in 1924 to 791 in 1927. With the advent of windrowing the number jumped to 4,448 in 1928 and to 9,562 in 1930. About two-thirds of the machines were in Saskatchewan, and most were in the prairie lands of the province rather than in the parklands. Farmers of large acreages adopted the combine first, generally favoring models with fifteen- or sixteen-foot headers, but, as smaller farmers also became owners, twelve-foot prairie models and ten-foot power-takeoff models became more prevalent. According to a

18

survey in 1928, 44 percent of the combine operators in western Canada practiced straight cutting only, while most of the rest both straight cut and picked up.[24]

Combiners in Canada also devised another invention to extend the use of the combine—the header-barge, used only to a limited extent in both Canada and the United States. The header-barge was a rick on skids that was drawn through the field beside a header and that received the cut grain from the header elevator. When it was filled, the driver tripped the rear slats to leave a great loaf of grain on the ground. The header and barge could be used as early in the season as the binder. Farmers threshed the stacks by driving a combine up next to them and pitching the grain onto the platform.[25]

Use of the combine proved practical in both the winter and spring wheat regions of the United States and Canada in the 1920s. Among winter wheat farmers harvesting with the combine was almost universal before 1940. For spring wheat farmers the transition to the combine was slower, arrested by depression during the 1930s. In 1938 a survey of eight counties across North Dakota showed that only about one-fourth of the wheat was harvested by combine, of which about one-half was windrowed and picked up and the other half was straight cut. Farmers in the eastern and northern portions of the state used the combine the least and, when they did, generally used the windrower also. Farmers in the western and southern parts of the state were more favorable to the combine and practiced straight cutting, but, even there, most still clung to the binder. In Kansas, on the other hand, conversion to the combine was nearly complete at this time. Almost nine-tenths of the wheat in eight sample counties was combined, nearly all by straight cutting, and in western counties as much as 99 percent was combined. Only continued use of the binder in some eastern counties kept down the total percentage of combined grain in the state. Thus, north and south, the combine was more prevalent on the high plains than in transitional areas just to the east. On the southern plains the combine had routed the army of harvest hands who previously had possessed the country, much to the delight of the farmers, who were released from the task of recruiting workers, and of the farmers' wives, who were freed from the burden of cooking for a harvest crew and from the worries of having strange and disreputable men about the place. Farther north large numbers of bindlestiffs still were needed—nearly 30,000 in North Dakota in 1938.[26]

Adoption of the combine brought changes in methods of farming. Its users found it necessary to "farm for the combine": to ensure even ripening, they sowed better seed at a uniform rate and at a consistent depth; to facilitate harvesting, they battled weeds and removed sticks, stones, and furrows from the fields. The combine also contributed to the evolution of larger farms on the plains and to the rapid mechanization of them. With the bottleneck of harvesting and threshing cleared, farmers expanded their acreage. They also purchased more tractors to pull the combines and to work the additional acres. Not only harvesting but also wheat farming in general became more capital-intensive with the advent of the combine.[27]

Effects on the organization and psychology of the harvest also were profound. Before the coming of the combine, harvesting was a more protracted process. Binding and heading started while the wheat was still green and continued after it was dead ripe. Threshing lasted all summer, as the custom threshing outfit moved from farm to farm in turn. This was little cause for worry, for grain in the stack was safe.

The combine made farmers more impatient and hasty. The wheat had to be combined quickly, as soon as it was ripe enough, whether it was standing or in the windrow. Delay meant possible losses from hail, lodging, or collapsed windrows and sure losses from shattering. Cooperative ownership of combines on the plains therefore was not feasible, for one owner would have to wait anxiously while the other's wheat was being combined.

The precedent for custom operation of costly machinery already had been established by threshermen, and so custom combining was a logical development. Often the same man who had owned a threshing rig was also an early owner of a combine in his locale. The owner of a combine generally first cut his own wheat and then combined for his neighbors. The other farmers kept their binders and headers in case the custom cutter was too late getting around to them. In some cases special types of custom work were available. Sometimes sawflies, hail, frost, or some other natural disaster either damaged crops so severely that it did not pay to bind and thresh them or else tangled the straw so badly that a binder could not tie bundles. Then farmers hired custom combiners to salvage what they could of the crop. There were reports from Alberta of combines saving from six to fifteen bushels of wheat to the acre in fields on which the government's crop insurance program already had paid 100 percent compensation for hail losses.[28]

Custom cutting on a local basis was prevalent wherever there were combines. The study of the combine on the Great Plains by the United States Department of Agriculture in 1926 found that more than half of the combine owners did custom work. This was of dual benefit: combine owners defrayed the cost of their machines with custom work, and farmers who hired out the cutting of their wheat got their crops harvested more cheaply than by other methods.

Rates received for custom combining varied with the number of combines competing for the business in the area. In Texas rates of $4.00 an acre were reported, and in Montana rates of $2.50, but the general price was about $3.00. Early in the harvesting season, farmers were willing to pay high rates for quick service, but competition from other combines drove the price down later in the harvest. At the going rate, and disregarding interest and depreciation, a custom cutter could net about $2.50 an acre for his work. Early custom cutting was a lucrative business.[29]

Separate reports for several individual states emphasized the importance of custom cutting in establishing the use of the combine. "The importance of custom cutting cannot be overestimated," said the report for Texas, "since it enables the owner of a combine to lower the cost of harvesting his own grain by earning enough to partially take care of the original investment."[30] In Texas one-third to one-half of the grain combined was custom cut. In Oklahoma more than two-thirds of the owners of prairie combines surveyed did custom work. In Montana about four-fifths of the combine owners did custom work, even including owners of power-takeoff models.[31]

Custom cutting at the local level became so profitable that some men with no small grains of their own to harvest bought combines just to do custom work. In 1927 the Schoelen Brothers, Henry and Frank, of Kingfisher County, Oklahoma, bought a combine, although they had no wheat of their own. By custom cutting 500 acres at $3.00 an acre, they paid for more than half the cost of the combine the first year. Cephus Rachliff of Major County represented a more common sort of part-time custom cutter. In 1927 he used his twenty-foot combine to cut his own 200 acres of wheat, and then he cut 400 acres more for his neighbors at $3.00 an acre. Financial terms for custom combining were not yet standardized. Most farmers paid a flat rate per acre for cutting, but some paid perhaps $1.50 an acre as a base rate and nine or ten cents a bushel in addition. One custom cutter, Henry Schuerman of Grant County, Oklahoma, agreed to cut wheat at a base rate of $3.00 an acre and five cents a bushel for every bushel more than twenty to the acre, a charge for high yields that foreshadowed what later would become a standard arrangement for custom rates. Sometimes farmers who were in the habit of paying for custom threshing by the bushel insisted on paying for custom combining the same way.[32]

A good example of a local custom cutter was Levi A. Quig, a slight, energetic farm boy from near Duquine in Harper County, southern Kansas. He bought his first combine in 1926, a twenty-foot No. 1 Rumely with a wooden header. He custom combined for farmers in the area, and he claimed his combine could cover eighty acres in a day. He charged $3.00 an acre, with no provision for high yields because there rarely were any. Unlike most custom cutters in those days, Quig contracted to haul the grain he cut to storage. He had a Model T truck with a homemade wooden bed and sideboards set out at the top to hold more grain, perhaps 100 or 125 bushels to a

Levi Quig (driving tractor) custom combined near Duquine, Kansas, in 1926 with his Rumely No. 1 combine and Rumely tractor. The farmer hauled his own grain by horse and wagon. *Photo courtesy of Levi Quig.*

load. He hauled grain to the elevator for three or four cents a bushel and to the bin for two cents.[33]

During the 1930s the low price of wheat depressed custom rates, but custom cutting went on. Charles Hildebrand, for instance, who lived just inside of Oklahoma south of Kiowa, Kansas, custom cut with a twelve-foot machine for his neighbors during those years. He had no truck to haul grain and received only $1.50 an acre for combining, but, by covering perhaps 400 acres in a season, he made a reasonable return for those days.[34]

During the 1930s, in fact, custom combining hesitantly entered a more extensive phase inspired by the progressive nature of the harvest from south to north. Although in any particular area the harvest was a brief affair, especially in the winter wheat region, for the Great Plains as a whole it lasted from the middle of May, when the first kernels hardened in northern Texas, until October or November, when snow erased the last windrows in Saskatchewan. It was logical that,

In 1927, Quig (standing beside header of front combine) had two Rumely combines and two Rumely tractors, and a farmer for whom he cut had a Model T Ford truck.
Photo courtesy of Levi Quig.

in order to get maximum use from expensive equipment, a few bold harvesters would attempt to transport their combines north with the harvest, becoming itinerant, professional custom cutters. The replacement of steel tires with rubber ones on combines and tractors made such a movement possible. Farmers as well as custom cutters benefited, for farmers employing traveling custom cutters no longer had to wait while some local combiner first finished his own wheat.

Quig, for instance, after a few years' experience custom cutting in southern Kansas, began to haul his combine to western Kansas after harvesting at home and make a second harvest in Lane County. Travel was slow, but in years when crops were poor at home, he supplemented his income this way. LeRoy Gregg of Hall County, Nebraska, was another traveling custom cutter. He began combining for neighbors in 1933,

and by 1938 he needed a new combine. The only way he could afford the price of $1,660 was to prolong the use of the machine, and since it was rubber-tired, he took it on the road. He took delivery of the new combine, a twelve-footer, at Enid, Oklahoma, and began harvesting there. He then worked his way north to Montana on a series of jobs, cutting his own wheat at home en route. It worked so well that thereafter he made it an annual trek.[35]

An outstanding and unusual example of an early traveling outfit was that assembled by A. J. Nickerson of Bushton, in central Kansas. Nickerson owned a garage in Bushton and also held franchises for Allis-Chalmers machinery and Firestone tires. So, although he was not a farmer, he had everything he needed to set up a custom outfit. Around 1929 he began custom cutting near Bushton and then making a second

This Rumely was one of the combines fielded by A. J. Nickerson during the 1930s. The header is detached and hitched behind the combine. The combine itself is hitched to Nickerson's "Buick tractor."
Photo courtesy of Joe Habiger.

harvest in Gove County, western Kansas. In the mid-1930s he added an earlier stop in southern Kansas, near Kiowa. His combines, three of them by 1940 or so, were Rumelys in sizes ranging up to twenty feet. Although the outfit took no trucks, Nickerson's mechanics refined methods of traveling with combines and tractors. The front wheel of each combine was lifted off the ground when hitched to the tractor to be towed on the road, and so the combines ran on two wheels and did not weave. The headers were detached and loaded on trailers hitched behind the combines. The Model E Allis-Chalmers tractor that led Nickerson's caravan made fifteen or twenty miles per hour on the road. One of the combines was hitched to what the men called the Buick tractor—a Buick automobile fitted with oversized tires and geared down so that it would pull a combine in the field, but still make thirty miles per hour on the highway.[36]

Some of the new traveling custom cutters were heirs of harvesting traditions already venerable in their families. One such was Everett Squires from Lenore, Oklahoma, in Dewey County west of Taloga. He was the son of Earl G. Squires, a farmer who in 1923 had surprised his neighbors by hauling home an Avery header-thresher all the way from Canton. The header-thresher was a forerunner of the combine, but amounted to little more than a light threshing machine hitched to receive the grain from the elevator of a header alongside. Squires used the machine not only to cut standing grain but also to thresh bound grain from the shock. He finished his own wheat in 1923 and then did custom work for his neighbors. For the sake of the manufacturers he issued a glowing testimonial: "We are using the Avery Header-Thresher with a sixteen foot header in wheat running 25 to 30 bushels to the acre and with long straw," he said. "The machine is absolutely all right and is running with the best of satisfaction to me." In

Thresherman Earl Squires brought this Avery header-thresher to Dewey County, Oklahoma, in 1923.
Photo courtesy of Everett and Mable Squires.

succeeding years Earl and Everett Squires did custom work also with stationary threshers and with combines.

In 1938, Everett first took combines on the road. His outfit included two Grainmaster 10 Oliver combines and two six-cylinder Chevrolet trucks. Few other outfits were on the road, but he met one using chain-drive trucks customized to pull twenty-four–foot Holt combines on the road and in the field. Squires took the business seriously from the start. His route the first year carried him to Altus, Thomas, Taloga, and Buffalo in Oklahoma, to Dodge City and Goodland in Kansas, and to Big Springs in Nebraska. Successful in early ventures, he quickly expanded operations. By 1942, Squires had seven Oliver combines ready for the highway.[37]

Traveling custom outfits in 1940 as yet harvested an insignificant portion of the wheat on the plains and attracted little attention. They were regarded as a picturesque, but temporary, phenomenon. In a study of the harvest in North Dakota in 1938 researchers from the United States Bureau of Agricultural Economics noted the presence of a few custom cutters from outside the state, but speculated that increased local ownership of combines soon would make such entrepreneurs superfluous.[38]

Still, interstate custom combining was remarkably suitable as a method of harvesting on the Great Plains. The progressive nature of the harvest from south to north and the increasing adaptability of combines to the highway made such a movement feasible. The need of farmers on the plains to obtain the benefits of the combine without suffering the hardship of a heavy capital investment made the movement desirable. The technology for an interstate custom combining industry was available, and the environment was suitable. All that was needed was some stimulation of the agricultural economy to precipitate the innovation. The First World War had helped to spark the adoption of the combine on the plains. Another world war also would prompt momentous changes in the harvest.

Chapter 2
Harvesting Heroes and Economic Opportunists 1942–47

"We are meeting here at a critical point in our world-wide war against dictatorship and aggression. It's our way of life or theirs," warned United States Secretary of Agriculture Claude R. Wickard.[1] He was addressing a meeting of wheat farmers in Enid, Oklahoma, on April 28, 1942. The theme of his speech was that patriotic farmers should attune their production to the needs of their country during wartime. The war brought radical changes to American agriculture. Not the least among these was a new system of harvesting wheat on the plains—interstate custom combining by professional harvesters. Custom cutters, as well as farmers, participated in the agricultural crusade called for by Wickard.

The initial effect of the war on wheat farming in the United States was misleading. Although there were immediate shortages of other products, the supply of wheat and small grains seemed more than sufficient, thanks to a decade of government commodity programs. In 1941 the United States had a carry-over of 400 million bushels of wheat from the previous year, most of it held by the Commodity Credit Corporation. Storage space in elevators was scarce, but enough room for the year's crop finally turned up: railroad officials shipped all available boxcars west; farmers built granaries on the farm; and elevator operators temporarily piled wheat on the ground when necessary.[2]

The situation in 1942 was even more perplexing, for the carry-over and crop both were larger than in 1941. When Wickard went to speak in Enid, it was not to ask wheat farmers to produce more, but to ask them to vote in favor of mandatory production quotas proposed by the Department of Agriculture. The quotas would enable the Commodity Credit Corporation to support the price at a reasonable level. "The job of American farmers is to produce more than they ever have produced before. But it must be more of the things that are needed," Wickard said. "We already have more wheat than we know what to do with."[3] He expected a crop of 800 million bushels to be added to a carry-over of 630 million bushels. The secretary told farmers to store as much wheat as possible in their own granaries—"Wallace's pillboxes," these were called in wartime—and to put their faith in government parity programs. In Canada during the same time, the government was unable to absorb surpluses or maintain the price.

Governmental efforts nevertheless were too effective in the light of subsequent developments. The grain reserves of the bulging ever-normal granary of the 1930s disappeared with unexpected quickness. As the United States government maintained a system of dual pricing that pegged wheat for feed at a price below that of wheat for flour, large quantities of wheat were fed to livestock. At the same time the governments of the United States and Canada made commitments to countries in western Europe to supply them with grain during reconstruction after the war. There was little difficulty in storing the crop of 1943, for not only had consumption been surprisingly high, but also the yield was lower than expected. The supply of wheat in the United States in the fall of 1942 had been 1.6 billion bushels, the largest in history, but the disappearance by 1943 also was the largest ever, totaling a billion bushels. The supply in the fall of 1943 was expected to be less than 1.4 billion bushels, with a much larger disappearance expected in the next year. In July officials of the Bureau of Agricultural Economics estimated that the supply of wheat would dwindle to what they considered a minimal reserve in a year.[4]

At that point the United States Department of Agriculture recognized the need for a rapid increase in production to meet immediate and postwar needs for grain. Commodity programs were maintained, but they were used to encourage production rather than to discourage it, guaranteeing farmers high prices for increased production. For 1944 the secretary of agriculture requested farmers in the Great Plains to seed 11 million acres more wheat than for 1943, an increase of nearly 10 percent. Farmers responded readily, whether because of patriotism or prices. Fields idle since the 1930s again were planted, summer fallow was decreased, and native sod on the high plains was turned under. Such practices continued for several years, until postwar demands for grain were satisfied in 1948.[5]

As production expanded, farmers tried to deal with what appeared to them to be a shortage of labor, although perhaps they merely had grown accustomed to having plentiful, cheap labor during the two decades previous. Conscription removed many potential workers, while the availability of employment in defense industries prevented any sizable exodus of laborers into the countryside for the harvest. The shortage of harvest workers was most severe in the spring wheat region, where the combine still was in only limited use. There the schoolchildren and the housewives mobilized to save the crops. Merchants and professional men turned out during evenings and weekends to blister their hands on pitchfork handles, often under the auspices of such organizations as the Rotary.[6]

The expansion of production and the shortage of labor led farmers to attempt to obtain laborsaving machinery, especially for harvesting, but they found such implements scarcer even than bindlestiffs. Steel was subject to strict rationing during the war, and although the war production boards of the United States and Canada allocated as much steel as possible to the manufacture of harvesting machinery, production trailed demand. Manufacturers produced 54,296 combines in the United States in 1941, but in 1942 the number dropped to 41,822, and in 1943 to 29,219. Only about one-tenth of the total production during these years consisted of combines of the size, ten-foot or larger, wanted by farmers on the plains.

31

Allocations of materials for agricultural implements in 1942 totaled just 80 percent of the amount used for the same purpose in 1940, and in 1943 only 40 percent.[7]

Such scarcities set off a scramble to obtain the few available combines. Already in 1942 farmers found that in many places harvesting machinery was unavailable except on the black market. The United States War Food Administration set up a rationing program for farm machinery in 1943. In order to buy any piece of equipment, a farmer first had to obtain a purchase certificate from his county war board, a local committee set up by the War Food Administration. The shortage of combines was severe in 1943, even before the great expansion in wheat production. Implement dealers on the southern plains bought used combines from farmers at top prices after the harvest there, often sending agents around to farms to bid on the machines. Then they shipped the combines north for resale in the Dakotas, where anxious farmers paid almost any price asked. One dealer from Kansas claimed to have shipped north twelve flatcars loaded with combines; a buyer from Oklahoma and a dealer in North Dakota arranged to market seventy combines; a dealer from Missouri dispatched 120 machines. Perhaps thousands of combines thus were shifted from south to north.[8]

The shortage intensified with the boom in wheat farming in 1944. The War Production Board eased strictures on the use of steel enough for manufacturers to produce 43,604 pull-type combines, 6,051 of them in sizes greater than ten feet, along with 1,100 self-propelled combines.[9] Unfortunately, few of these were available early in the harvest. This caused problems particularly for farmers on the southern plains who had sold their combines to dealers for resale in the north, believing that new machines would be ready for them in 1944. The situation perhaps was only just deserts for such careless profiteers, but the country needed their wheat anyway. Shortages and dislocations in the supply of combines eased only gradually until by 1948 production had caught up with demand.

A result of all these circumstances in the years 1942 through 1947 was the rapid development of interstate custom combining, an arrangement that eased shortages and saved farmers from losses. Custom combining was the one measure short of ownership and operation of combines by the government that could obtain the fullest possible use of the implement in short supply. A class of mobile professional harvesters developed during and after the war. In some ways they were like the bindlestiffs who earlier had ranged the length of the plains and who still were important in the spring wheat region. They had the same mobility, and they provided farmers with seasonal labor. In other respects the custom cutters were like the threshermen, furnishing capital and expertise for hire along with workers. Yet the custom cutters were a new sort of entrepreneur, neither as footloose as the bindlestiffs, who had only their own strong arms to offer and only their own selves to care for, nor as parochial as the threshermen, who never left their own localities.

Stalwarts of the movement were the few harvesters who had begun traveling with their machines during the 1920s or 1930s, like Quig, Gregg, Nickerson, and Squires. They generally expanded their activities during and immediately after the war, adding to their machinery, working a longer season, or both. Levi Quig, the custom cutter from Duquine, Kansas, lengthened his route to include not only southern and western Kansas but also the Nebraska Panhandle. LeRoy Gregg of Nebraska bought a second combine in 1942; thus his outfit included two tractors, two grain trucks, and two panel trucks. From Oklahoma he worked north to Saskatchewan, where he harvested until December. The next year, with workers scarce, he added his two teenage daughters to his crew as truck drivers. Before the season was finished he had acquired a third combine and had worked his way through North Dakota and Montana. A. J. Nickerson's outfit from Bushton, Kansas, sporting its three Rumely combines, began to cover an impressive harvesting circuit—to Kingman, Bushton, and Grinnell in Kansas, on to Bird City and Alliance in Nebraska, next to Martin in South Dakota, and finally to Mott and Minot in North Dakota. The tour comprised nine stops and ended in a homeward drive of 700 miles.[10]

Everett Squires of Taloga, Oklahoma, in particular was ready to exploit the situation during the war. He already owned seven Oliver combines and seven trucks that he had accumulated in the years preceding the war, before the price of machinery went up. Although classified 1-A by the Selective Service, he received a deferment in order to continue custom cutting. During the early 1940s, Squires employed a crew of seventeen to nineteen men each year. He already had as large an outfit as he could handle and covered a lengthy route, but in 1946 he began the conversion of his fleet to self-propelled combines, purchasing two that year.[11]

Thousands of newcomers joined these pioneers and made custom combining an important part of the agricultural economy of the Great Plains. The swelling of the movement started in 1942, as shortages of machinery and labor began. During 1942 and 1943 the increase was more dramatic, as the harvest assumed a tone of emergency, patriotism, and oppor-

A custom outfit from Weatherford, Texas, on the Elmer Graffis farm, Seibert, Colorado, in 1946 loads the machines on trailers to haul north to the next stop.
Photo courtesy of Elmer Graffis.

34

Five Massey-Harris No. 21 custom combines cut wheat for Elmer Graffis in 1946.
Photo courtesy of Elmer Graffis.

tunism. At the close of the war in 1945, and in the postwar years of 1946 and 1947, custom cutting continued to increase. Shortages of machinery eased, but high prices for grain kept the combines for hire busy. Farmers also bought their own machines during the flush times, however, and when the price of grain broke in 1948, custom cutters suffered. Like farmers, they had expanded to excess during prosperous times.

Statistics compiled by various governmental agencies during the years of expansion testified to the growth of custom cutting. In 1942 the business was significant enough that the United States Bureau of Agricultural Economics launched a study of custom combine outfits in Nebraska. Agents of the Motor Fuels Division of the Nebraska Department of Revenue, while checking incoming custom cutters for the amount of gasoline they were bringing in, collected information for

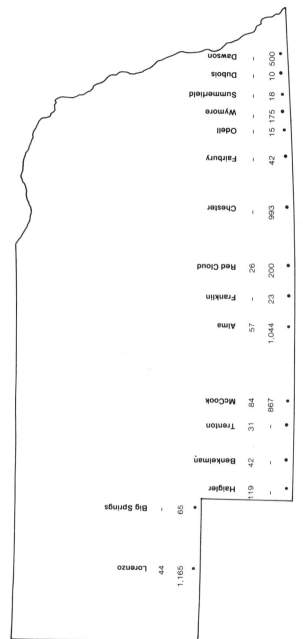

Fig. 1. Custom combines registered at ports of entry in Nebraska, 1942 and 1947. Top number is number of combines registered in 1942; bottom number is number registered in 1947. Data from Noxious Weeds Division, Bureau of Plant Industry, Nebraska State Department of Agriculture.

the study at seven ports of entry. Officials of the Noxious Weed Control Division of the Nebraska Department of Agriculture, while traveling the state to prevent harvesters from inadvertently spreading weeds with their machines, interviewed a few more custom cutters. An unknown number of custom cutters in the state missed being interviewed: those who passed through a port of entry on the southern border not manned by revenue agents, those who entered the state from the north, east, or west, and those who ran the ports of entry at night to avoid inspections all escaped detection, unless a roving weed inspector happened to catch up with them. Also, outfits that had originated in Nebraska, gone south, and were returning home were not subject to inspections at ports of entry. Weed inspectors gathered information on a few of these within the state, however.

The researchers managed to catch up with 447 custom combines (see Figure 1). They treated each combine and the machinery and men associated with it as a unit for the collection of data, for at that time hardly any custom cutters owned more than one machine. Nearly one-half of the combines for which a place of origin was recorded came from Kansas, almost one-fourth from Oklahoma, and about one-tenth from Texas (see Figure 2). These data indicated that the southern plains was the great cradle of custom cutters in the industry's first year of expansion. Few custom cutters yet came from the northern plains. Some Dakotans may have escaped the count by entering Nebraska from the north, but these probably were few. If a northern custom cutter meant to venture into the winter wheat region, he would have gone at least as far south as Kansas. Combines from the southern plains also tended to be larger models than those from other areas. Because the study did not cover all ports of entry, it offered little definite information on what areas of Nebraska had the most custom cutters, but, since state officials chose to monitor mostly western ports of entry, they must have expected the greatest numbers of combines there. As anticipated, the port of entry at Haigler, in the southwest corner of the state, registered more combines than any other port.[12]

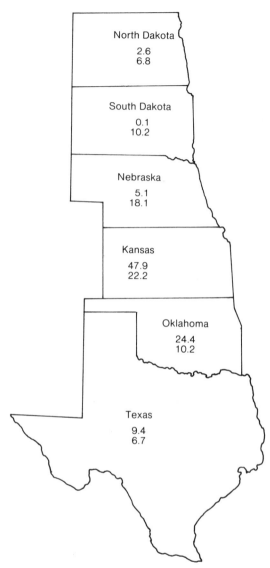

Fig. 2. Principal states of origin for custom combines (1942) and custom combine outfits (1947) in Nebraska. Top number is percentage of combines originating in a state in 1942; bottom number is percentage of outfits originating in a state in 1947. Data from Hecht, *Transient Combine-Harvester-Threshers in the Great Plains, 1942;* and Leker, *Farm Labor Program for Wheat and Other Small Grain Harvest in the Great Plains States, 1943 to 1947.*

A second survey of custom cutters in Nebraska done in 1947 showed that their business had flourished in the course of five years. This time representatives of the Agricultural Extension Service and officials of the ports of entry covered thirteen ports along the southern border of the state, but, no doubt, they still overlooked some outfits passing through other southern ports or entering from the north, east, or west. In this case outfits from Nebraska also were counted if they were coming home from another state. The researchers found 5,117 combines entering thirteen ports, as opposed to 515 counted at seven ports in 1942 (see Figure 1). Some of the ports covered in 1942 were neglected in the study of 1947, and many manned in 1947 had been overlooked in 1942. Nevertheless, it was plain that a great increase in traffic had occurred. Ports at which counts were made in both 1942 and 1947—Alma, McCook, and Lorenzo—registered tenfold and twentyfold increases in the number of combines entering. The wheat regions of the south-central and far western parts of the state attracted the greatest numbers of machines, but the 500 combines that entered at Dawson, in the southeastern corner of the state, showed that the movement was not confined to the high plains.

Information about the places of origin of custom cutters in Nebraska in 1947 showed that although combiners from the southern plains still were predominant, harvesters from the northern plains also were entering the field (see Figure 2). Unlike the researchers in 1942, those in 1947 recorded place of origin by outfit, not by individual combine. More outfits still came from Kansas than from any other state, but Kansas's share of the total had shrunk to about one-fifth of 2,969 outfits. Nebraskans rivaled Kansans as custom cutters in Nebraska. Canada and South Dakota each contributed more outfits than Oklahoma did, while North Dakota sent more than Texas.[13]

During about the same period of years, custom combining underwent a similar boom in South Dakota, where both winter and spring wheat were grown. In 1943 the supervisor of farm labor for the extension service in South Dakota asked of-

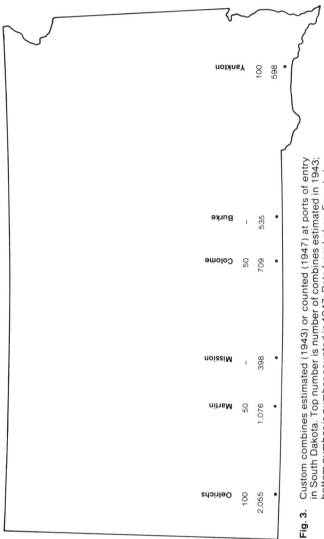

Fig. 3. Custom combines estimated (1943) or counted (1947) at ports of entry in South Dakota. Top number is number of combines estimated in 1943; bottom number is number counted in 1947. Data from Leker, *Farm Labor Program for Wheat and Other Small Grain Harvest in the Great Plains States, 1943 to 1947.*

ficials at the ports of entry on the southern border of the state to estimate the number of combines entering through their ports. The estimates from the six ports of entry totaled only 300. In 1947 all combines entering the state were required to stop and be registered at the ports of entry, and so an accurate count was made except for those custom cutters who may have run the ports of entry. The combines registered numbered 6,370 (see Figure 3). As in the case of Nebraska, the greatest numbers arrived through western ports of entry, especially Oelrichs, but hundreds came through even as far east as Yankton.[14]

Similar returns from Kansas showed that, although custom cutting was flourishing at the end of World War II, the business continued to expand immediately after the war. Officials at all ports of entry on the southern border of the state made counts or close estimates of the numbers of combines entering the state each year from 1945 through 1947. In 1945 they said 3,145 combines entered the state; in 1946 the number nearly doubled, reaching 6,248; in 1947 continued expansion pushed the total to 8,048 (see Figure 4). There probably were many combines that entered Kansas from the north to begin custom harvesting. Also, combines originating in Kansas that went south to harvest and returned home were not counted at the ports of entry. In 1945, for instance, officials of the Extension Service estimated that 525 combines went south from Kansas and returned, and that 500 combines entered Kansas from the north to start their harvesting season, including 250 from Canada.[15]

Each year from 1945 to 1947 the Extension Service in most states of the Great Plains required their county agents to report the number of custom combines employed in their counties. Some agents reported only those custom outfits that they placed on jobs themselves, while others estimated the total number of custom combines at work in their counties. Many custom outfits, because they worked in several areas in one state, were counted repeatedly. Nevertheless, the totals compiled by the extension services from reports by their county agents gave rough testimony to the growth of custom

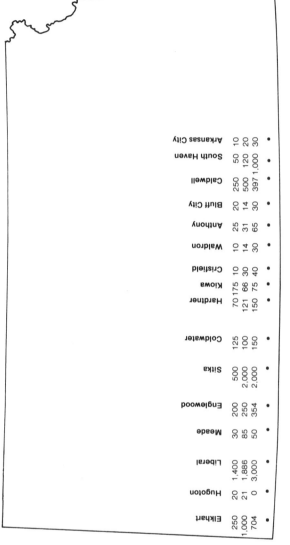

Fig. 4. Custom combines registered (or estimated) at ports of entry in Kansas, 1945–47. Top number is number of combines in 1945; second number is number of combines in 1946; bottom number is number of combines in 1947. Data from Leker, *Farm Labor Program for Wheat and Other Small Grain Harvest in the Great Plains States, 1943 to 1947.*

Port of entry	1945	1946	1947
Elkhart	250	1,000	704
Hugoton	20	21	0
Liberal	1,400	1,886	3,000
Meade	30	85	50
Englewood	200	250	354
Sitka	500	2,000	2,000
Coldwater	125	100	150
Hardtner	70	121	150
Kiowa	175	66	75
Crisfield	10	30	40
Waldron	10	14	30
Anthony	25	31	65
Bluff City	20	14	30
Caldwell	250	500	397
South Haven	50	120	1,000
Arkansas City	10	20	30

Table 1.

Custom Combines and Trucks from out of Area as Reported by County Extension Agents, 1945–47

State	Combines			Trucks		
	1945	1946	1947	1945	1946	1947
Texas	2,895	5,097	9,138	1,815	1,312	5,537
Oklahoma	1,521	1,680	2,781	3,000	3,500	3,645
Kansas	5,779	5,236	7,800	4,790	3,256	5,084
Colorado			1,476			1,072
Nebraska	1,500	3,030	2,681	1,000	1,801	1,777
South Dakota	1,000	2,656	3,560	500	1,000	2,100
North Dakota	1,634	1,637	2,958	2,816	2,642	3,865

Source: Leker, *Farm Labor Program for Wheat and Other Small Grain Harvest in the Great Plains States, 1943 to 1947.*

cutting (see Table 1). Each state showed increasing use of custom cutters through the three years. In Texas the increase was spectacular, more than 300 percent, making the farmers of Texas the greatest employers of custom cutters in 1947.[16]

The rapid expansion of custom combining in the mid-1940s was evident in individual experiences as well as in aggregate information. Perhaps the best-known custom outfit of the early years of the business was that of Norman R. Hamm of Cheney, Kansas. He assembled a caravan of machinery and a crew of men so impressive that it generally was known as "Hammtown." Hamm started custom cutting with a small drag machine for his neighbors in 1940 and went on the road in 1942, the first year of the boom in the business. Rapid growth of the industry affected his outfit accordingly: by 1947 his harvesting caravan included eight trucks towing eight self-propelled Massey-Harris combines. On arriving at a new job, Hamm's men immediately unloaded the combines and cut an acre or two to accommodate a village of trailers—two sleepers, a cookshack, a service trailer, a shower, a recreation trailer, and a baggage trailer. From Texas to North Dakota,

43

Hamm's outfit cut a wide swath—400 or 500 acres for each full day of cutting.[17]

Expansion did not have to be on such a grand scale. John Stephenson of Coon Rapids, Iowa, ran a modest operation designed to supplement his income from farming. He owned a twelve-foot drag combine with pickup header to harvest his own 150 acres of small grains. In 1946, on finishing combining at home, he headed for Jamestown, North Dakota, to make a second harvest. He handled the combine himself, hired the neighbor's boys to drive his truck and tractor, and left the chores at home to his teenage son. He repeated the venture in 1947. Although each year he harvested only a few hundred acres, Stephenson added one more machine to the ranks of interstate custom cutters.[18]

Many other custom harvesters also operated small outfits, but ranged over more territory than did Stephenson. Fred Brown had a wheat farm near Clinton, Oklahoma, and when custom combining began to boom, he saw an opportunity to augment his income. In 1945 he and his seventeen-year-old son, Jim, took their drag machine on a short run northward. Then they invested their profits in a new Massey-Harris self-propelled combine. After finishing their own wheat in 1946, the two traveled to Dodge City and Oakley in Kansas and to Alliance in Nebraska, harvesting about 1,300 acres and heading home at the end of July with about $2,000 in net earnings. Such success meant another recruit to the army of custom cutters.[19]

Working on a similar scale was Ted Hardwick of Saxmon in south-central Kansas. In his locale farms were relatively small, diversified operations, and Hardwick accordingly began custom cutting on a small scale. In 1942 he bought his first combine, a nine-foot drag Minneapolis Moline. He cut his own 200 acres of wheat with the little Minnie and then custom cut for his neighbors for $3.00 an acre. The next year he traded for a seven-foot Massey-Harris Clipper combine, a model designed for the Midwest. He cut wheat for himself and his neighbors in the summer and custom cut 200 acres of milo in the fall, two rows at a time. In 1944, the methodical

Hardwick bought a fourteen-foot drag John Deere combine, and finally, in 1947, as the boom in custom combining reached its peak, he invested in a self-propelled John Deere. Local small farmers scoffed at his $4,700 investment, but soon they were hiring him to open fields for them for twenty-five cents a bushel. That year Hardwick traveled to western Kansas to seek additional work—another convert to a growing profession.[20]

Some even abandoned defense work to become custom combiners. W. H. Ring, who grew up on a farm in Harper County, Kansas, left a job in Oklahoma City at the onset of World War II to work in an airplane assembly plant in Wichita. After only a few months he tired of indoor work. In the spring of 1942, Ring obtained a purchase certificate and bought a small drag Oliver combine for $1,410 in Newton. Then he headed for Alva, Oklahoma, to begin harvesting. His travels that year carried him to Sedgwick and Dighton in Kansas, to Sutherland and Potter in Nebraska, and to Baker in Montana, and he found work all the way. He sold his combine to a farmer in Montana and went home, but the next year he was back in the harvest with a drag Massey-Harris machine, starting in Mountain View, Oklahoma, and finishing in Wagner, South Dakota. Each year thereafter Ring made the harvest. He got his first self-propelled combines in 1945, leasing three Massey-Harris No. 21As.[21]

Implement dealers made up another group that entered eagerly into custom combining, by sending machines from their own inventories on the road, often under the management of a trusted employee. Paul Swanson of Devil's Lake, North Dakota, was one of these enterprising dealers. He first sent combines into the harvest in 1942, when the two Massey-Harris machines he dispatched started cutting at Enid, Oklahoma. These machines had paid for themselves before they had left Kansas. By 1947, Swanson had sent as many as seven combines into Oklahoma, sometimes netting profits as high as $5,000 per machine.[22]

Joe Vater was another custom-cutting implement dealer. Diminutive, businesslike Vater later was to become known as the foremost salesman of Allis-Chalmers Gleaner combines in the world. He acquired the Gleaner-Baldwin dealership in Enid in 1945. That same year he transported a Model E Gleaner combine to Syracuse, Kansas, to custom cut with Anthony O'Brate, an acquaintance from Syracuse. For years thereafter Vater took four Model Es to western Kansas and western Nebraska to work with O'Brate, but then he gave up the practice in order to devote more attention to his dealership.[23]

The great increase in custom combining in the years 1942 through 1947 came about mostly because of the actions of individual entrepreneurs like Vater and the rest. In one notable case, however, custom cutting received a boost from the carefully planned, highly publicized efforts of an implement company. This was the case of the Massey-Harris Self-propelled Harvest Brigade of 1944.

In the fall of 1943, when the governments of the United States and Canada called on farmers for the greatest increases in wheat production, farmers wondered how they were to harvest the increased acreage. Production of farm machinery was at its lowest level because of quotas on materials, and farm labor was scarce because of inductions into the armed forces and the attractions of defense work. Governmental officials shared the concern of farmers. This gave Massey-Harris Company the chance not only to assist in an agricultural emergency, but also to bring in favorable publicity.

Massey-Harris Company, with its principal plant in Toronto, Ontario, and a subsidiary in Racine, Wisconsin, was the world's leading manufacturer of harvesting implements. In 1939 the company had released its No. 20 self-propelled combine, the first practical self-propelled combine, which was used by a few Canadian farmers in the harvest of 1940. The company then released an improved movel, the No. 21, just in time to begin production before the Canadian government prohibited the introduction of new models for the duration of the war.[24]

Joseph Tucker, vice-president of sales for the company's subsidiary in Racine, earlier had served on the War Production Board of the United States. He had been the board's liaison with the War Production Board of Canada. To his colleagues in the company and his acquaintances in the government, Tucker proposed that the No. 21 combine be used to save the harvest of 1944. The plan he had in mind required the approval of both governments, and so Tucker went to Washington, while other lobbyists for the company went to Ottawa.

They urged that the Massey-Harris plant in Toronto be granted an extra allocation, above its established quota, of enough steel and other materials to make 500 No. 21 combines. The company then was to place these machines in the hands of custom combiners in areas where they were needed in 1944. Tucker obtained support for the plan from Marvin Jones, administrator of the United States War Production Board, and Jones requested his Canadian counterparts to grant the company's request. They did. While workers started the extra combines down the assembly line, officials of the company made plans for the coming harvest and announced the formation of the Massey-Harris Self-propelled Harvest Brigade.[25]

Their plan was to deliver the combines as they became available to four general areas of need. Some were to go to the west coast for the California Brigade, which would begin by harvesting flax in southern California and end up combining wheat in the central part of the state. Others would make up a Pacific Northwest Brigade for the wheat harvest there. Still more were to form a Southern Brigade in southern Texas, harvesting flax and oats, and then swing north and west into the wheat harvest, except for those machines remaining in Texas to harvest milo. The great majority of the combines were to go to Kansas and Oklahoma for a Central Plains Brigade, which would cut its way north through the winter wheat and spring wheat regions.[26]

In February, 1944, representatives of Massey-Harris Company met with groups of experienced custom cutters in towns up and down the wheat belt—places like Hastings, Nebraska, Watertown, South Dakota, and Topeka, Kansas. The spokesmen explained that Massey-Harris would distribute 500 No.

21 combines with fourteen-foot headers through dealers across the plains. To join the Harvest Brigade, a custom cutter was to consult his local dealer, who would accompany him to the office of his county war board to obtain a purchase certificate for a combine. The custom cutter then was to pay cash for the machine, but he was to take delivery of it at the place where he planned to begin harvesting. For members of the Central Plains Brigade, this usually meant a place like Enid or Altus, Oklahoma, or Hutchinson, Kansas. Each custom cutter was to declare his "unqualified intention" to cut 2,000 acres of grain with each machine and was to forward records of his operations to the offices of Massey-Harris Company.[27]

Finding plenty of custom cutters eager to buy the 500 combines, the company went ahead with its plans and publicity. Brochures and news releases emphasized the patriotic contribution the Harvest Brigade would make, but also pointed out the virtues of the No. 21 combine. The No. 21, they claimed, would cut fifty acres in a day, compared to forty acres for a drag machine of the same size. Each self-propelled combine used in place of a drag machine would release a tractor and a man for other work. A self-propelled combine would consume less fuel than would a tractor and a combine with auxiliary engine and would save grain that otherwise would be lost in opening fields. The company announced a goal for the Harvest Brigade of a million acres cut, based on an expectation of 2,000 acres for each of 500 combines.[28]

The Harvest Brigade, true to its name, took shape with mock-military organization. The head of Massey-Harris in Racine was the general of the Harvest Brigade. Each regional branch manager became a colonel, each territorial manager a major, and each local dealer a captain. Massey-Harris mechanics received the lowly rank of technical sergeant. Bulwarks of the brigade, of course, were its lieutenants, the custom cutters. The company appropriated $8,000 for "decorations"—war bonds of from $100 to $500. Each custom cutter was to mail his receipts for harvesting to the company as he accumulated them, and at harvest's end, the custom cutters who had done the most work (as measured by dollar receipts) would receive the bonds as prizes.[29]

In April the first combines of the Harvest Brigade, having completed their journey from Toronto, rolled off railroad flatcars in southern Texas, there to churn into fields of ripe flax. Meanwhile hundreds of grain trucks from all over the plains converged on points of delivery for combines of the Central Plains Brigade. The custom cutters fired up their machines in time to join forces with the Southern Brigade. A clattering, crimson arc stretching from the Cross Timbers to the Rocky Mountains, these self-styled panzers of the prairies would pursue the harvest north to the Canadian border and beyond.

Once in the field, the custom cutters benefited from efficient joint planning by Massey-Harris Company and the United States Agricultural Extension Service. County extension agents and Massey-Harris dealers labored to bring together custom cutters needing jobs and farmers needing harvesters. Often they set up temporary offices at grain elevators or implement dealerships and ranged into the countryside to inquire about farmers' needs. Ahead of the advancing brigade, in the company's airplanes, flew representatives who scouted out the ripeness of the wheat and the supply of combines. The company also sent truckloads of parts and delegations of servicemen into the field to answer calls for help, repairmen sometimes hastening to a point of trouble by airplane. Oil companies sent tank trucks of fuel into the fields. Officials of the Agricultural Extension Service, the Agricultural Adjustment Administration, and the War Food Administration made sure that harvesters received sufficient supplies of gasoline and tires.[30]

Some difficulties arose. It became apparent that a few inexperienced harvesters had slipped into the ranks to bedevil the company's mechanics. Dealers in the southern plains complained of difficulties in keeping operators from the northern plains, less knowledgeable about combines, in action. Nevertheless, early reports from the field were better than expected, and by the middle of summer, spokesmen for Massey-

Harris Company announced that they had increased the goal of the Harvest Brigade to a million and a half acres. This proved too optimistic. The performance of the harvesters deteriorated later in the year, due to attrition from the ranks and to the usual tendency for the harvest to slow down in the spring wheat region. The total number of acres cut was 1,019,500. The Harvest Brigade threshed better than 25,000,000 bushels of grain for more than 5,000 farmers. The champion combiner was Wilford Phelps of Chandler, Arizona, who cut 3,438 acres and won a $500 war bond. Massey-Harris Company was a bigger winner: it released a color motion picture entitled *Wonder Harvest* to extoll the glories of the Harvest Brigade and the No. 21 combine.[31]

The fanfare attendant to the Harvest Brigade only emphasized the more profound change in wheat harvesting that had occurred in the early 1940s. The men of the Harvest Brigade were the shock troops of a larger force. A new industry had been founded, and although few realized it at the time, it possessed the traits of mobility and flexibility necessary for success on the plains. Custom combining was an admirable adaptation, one long overdue, finally ushered into existence by the exigencies of war.

Chapter 3
**Hard Times and
Painful Adjustments
1948–77**

Even as the boom in custom combining unfolded during
World War II, many observers predicted that it was a passing
phenomenon and that, once the emergency had ended, farmers would resume harvesting their own grain. For manufacturers of farm implements, this was wishful thinking. If
custom cutters harvested much of the grain, making each
combine cover more acres, then fewer combines would be
purchased. Executives of Massey-Harris Company, architects
of the self-propelled combine and the Harvest Brigade, were
in an uncomfortable position in relation to their fellows in the
business. The self-propelled combine was well suited to custom combining because of its speed of operation, ease of
transport, and economy of labor. (Conservative farmers, on
the other hand, disliked the innovation because it replicated
machinery. A farmer had to own a tractor anyway, they said,
and so he might as well use it to draw a combine.) Massey-
Harris seemed to be promoting its new self-propelled combines at the expense of the eventual welfare of the implement
industry. Joe Tucker acknowledged that his Harvest Brigade
might have opened a Pandora's box for the implement mak-
ers, but he reassured them, "I don't believe there is much to
fear of custom combining becoming very popular under nor-
mal economic conditions."[1]

Some farmers agreed. "Sure we hired our wheat custom
cut during the war," said one from the Oklahoma Panhandle,
"but as soon as we could get a new combine after the war we
got it and hope to cut all of our own wheat from now on."[2]

Many were puzzled when during the first couple of years after the war, custom cutting failed to die out as it was supposed to. This they attributed to the continued shortage of machinery. Most machinery manufacturers, wheat farmers, and government officials still considered custom combining an annual phenomenon. They assumed that each spring custom cutters surveyed the agricultural situation for the coming year—the acreage planted, the yield expected, and the ability of farmers to pay for harvesting—and then responded to the need, if any, for custom cutters. They failed to realize that a new class of men had been created, professional custom cutters, to whom harvesting had become as much a way of life as farming was to their customers. These men were emotionally attached to their occupation, and they had capital invested in it. They would enter the harvest even if prospects were dismal, just as farmers would plant their wheat even if the price was poor. Although the late 1940s brought hard times for custom cutters, their business survived to become an established agricultural institution on the plains. Seeded as an annual to meet an emergency, custom cutting evolved into a perennial.

Hard times for custom cutters began in 1948. The cause of their troubles was a sudden break in the price of wheat, as the postwar, international shortage of grain ended. The miraculous expansion of production, earlier hailed as a patriotic effort, eventually brought price-depressing surpluses. From the Agriculture Act of 1948 to the Food and Agriculture Act of 1977, the United States government implemented a variety of policies to deal with the problem of chronic overproduction of wheat. For custom cutters, the significance of most of these programs was that they were designed to limit marketings or acreage of wheat. With production restricted, farmers had less need for custom cutters. They were reluctant to employ custom cutters anyway when the price of wheat was low, preferring instead to make do with what machinery they had or to trade work with neighbors.

Compounding the problem in 1948 were hundreds of custom combining novices who made the harvest for the first time, attracted by tales of profits in previous years. In 1948,

Table 2.

Custom Cutters Entering Nebraska From out of State,
as Reported by the Nebraska State Employment
Service, 1948–60

Year	Outfits	Machines	Men
1948		4,866	
1949		[more than 4,000]	
1950		2,664	
1951		1,251	
1952	1,985	2,860	
1953	2,696	4,176	7,682
1954	2,482	3,960	7,416
1955	1,913	2,969	5,838
1956	2,347	3,833	7,025
1957		3,773	
1958		6,868	
1959		5,031	
1960		6,296	

Source: Annual Farm Labor Reports of the Nebraska State Employment Service.

and for years afterward, the Nebraska State Employment Service registered custom cutters entering the state at five principal ports of entry, recording information on an estimated 70 or 75 percent of combiners coming in. Whereas the Agricultural Extension Service, in a blanket of thirteen ports of entry, had registered 5,117 combines in 1947, the state employment service counted nearly as many, 4,866, at just the five ports of entry it covered in 1948 (see Table 2).[3]

Custom cutters who had cultivated a clientele of farmers they served year after year survived the season in good shape, but newcomers to the business met with disaster. The supply of combines in 1948 exceeded demand up and down the plains. Combines stood silent in the streets and alleys of small towns, representing not only unproductive capital, but also idle workers who kept right on eating whether they worked or not. The carefree days when a few good old boys could form a custom outfit and make enough money in the summer to last them the rest of the year were over.

As the harvest of 1948 moved across the southern plains, weather temporarily disguised the surplus of combines. Although machines stood idle in many communities, in other isolated areas there were brief shortages. This was because the wheat matured early in northern Kansas and southern Nebraska, and combines flowed to those areas, leaving uncut wheat behind. The oversupply became apparent in Nebraska in the middle of July. Nebraska was and is liable to chronic surpluses of combines because the wheat belt narrows in the northern part of the state, funneling custom cutters into a small area where there is not enough work for all. Custom cutters made camp to wait for wheat to be ready farther north, but conditions there were no better. During harvest the North Dakota State Employment Service announced a standing surplus of 500 combines, about one-third the number of machines that entered from out of state. The employment service also reported more intrastate custom combiners working in the state than interstate ones, indicating that farmers were hiring neighbors with combines to pick up their wheat rather than harvesters from outside the state. In previous years many custom cutters had sold their machines at inflated prices to farmers in North Dakota at the end of the year. This time few farmers bought. Custom cutters who had made the long trip from Oklahoma or Kansas were hard put to scrape up enough money to get home. In pawn shops and on streets they peddled tools and tires for cash to buy gas.[4]

The poor conditions continued in 1949, for the number of custom combines still did not decrease enough to match demand. According to the records, 5,449 combines were cleared through ports of entry along the southern border of Kansas; officials of the state employment service there estimated that between 6,000 and 7,000 went north from the state; inspectors at five ports of entry on the southern border of Nebraska counted more than 4,000 machines. Again the

Table 3.

Custom Combines Entering North Dakota From
out of State, as Reported by the North Dakota
State Employment Service, 1948–51

Year	Combines
1948	1,215
1949	1,082
1950	957
1951	486

Source: Annual Farm Labor Reports of the North Dakota
State Employment Service.

surplus of combines was particularly severe in Nebraska and
little better farther north. Although the number of combines
venturing as far as North Dakota declined slightly, there still
were several hundred more than needed (see Table 3). Harvest had no more than begun in neighboring Montana before
a surplus of anxious custom cutters was reported there, too.[5]

Two years of depressed conditions brought adjustments for
the industry. During flush years many farmers had bought
their own machines, enabling them to spurn custom cutters'
services. Farmers, especially in the spring wheat regions, demanded not complete outfits but skilled workers to drive
their machines. Discouraged by the economic situation and
by unusually heavy rains, custom cutters were less numerous
during the harvests of 1950 and 1951 than in previous years.
The state employment services of both Nebraska and North
Dakota reported fewer custom combines in 1950 and fewer
still in 1951. Custom combining had reached its lowest ebb,
but, from a broader point of view, the business had made the
necessary adjustment to reduced demand. Custom cutting
was at least a more flexible institution than wheat farming, on
which it was based. Although custom cutters reacted to a depressed market only slowly, causing hard times temporarily,
within a few years the ranks thinned. A hard core of professionals stayed in the business, acquiring further emotional at-

tachments and additional debts to prevent them from leaving even if they wanted to; marginal operators dropped out.[6]

In 1952 the business began a new period of growth. Custom cutting produced no quick profits in the 1950s, but neither did wheat farming. As the market for wheat bottomed out, it was apparent that the surplus of grain was chronic, not temporary. Yet for wheat farmers on the plains there was little alternative to raising wheat, since their land was poorly adapted for anything else. Lacking the flexibility of cropping that farmers enjoyed in regions of greater diversification, some wheat farmers on the plains took up custom combining as an adjunct to their grain farming, just as other farmers might expand their livestock feeding or take part-time jobs in town. Nearly all custom cutters were part-time farmers, part-time harvesters.

The harvest of 1952 showed that although many custom harvesters had left the business during hard times, they were quick to return when conditions merited it. Acreage had expanded only slightly over the previous year, but yields were much higher, slowing the progress of the harvest and requiring more combines. The weather was hot and dry on the central plains. All the wheat seemed to ripen at once. To everyone's surprise, a shortage of combines developed in Kansas. The state employment service, caught flat-footed, issued appeals for harvesters to load up their machines and come to Kansas. More important, farmers with cash in hand awaited custom cutters in every town. Combines flowed in rapidly from surrounding states to bring in the crop. As the harvesting minutemen who had come to Kansas's relief moved on north, they caused a surplus of machines in Nebraska, but most were sensible enough to go home from there rather than try their luck in the spring wheat region. Demand for custom combines was light in North Dakota, as in previous years.[7]

Apparently, the flurry of activity in Kansas in 1952 encouraged many marginal custom cutters to make the harvest in 1953. There were plenty of combines in the area in which they had been scarce the previous year, and in Nebraska, as more combines poured in to harvest a smaller crop, there was a large surplus. Once again most of the extra combiners turned around and went home from Nebraska; only about the number needed went to North Dakota. Likewise, in 1954 there were too many combines in parts of the central plains, this time because drought decreased the amount of wheat to harvest. Reductions in the numbers of combines on the road in 1955 and 1956 finally brought supply into line with demand again.[8]

The cycle of expansion and contraction then repeated itself. In 1957 temporary forces drew additional custom cutters into the harvest. Cutting in Oklahoma was delayed, for heavy rains caused lodging and made fields muddy. Many custom cutters pulled out of the state to meet commitments farther north. Hot weather then dried the fields of Oklahoma and ripened the wheat in Kansas and Nebraska all at the same time. While combines were spread thin across Kansas, farmers in Oklahoma cried for machines to return. An early harvest in Nebraska produced shortages of combines even there. By the time custom cutters moved into Nebraska, rains began again, holding combines there until harvest farther north was in full swing, and there was a shortage of combines. Because of the foul weather, fewer than one-third as many custom cutters reached Montana as in the previous year.[9]

The apparent shortages of combines in 1957 really were only dislocations, but they attracted additional custom cutters into the harvest of 1958. Fortunately, a record crop of winter wheat put the newcomers to profitable use, even in Nebraska. In 1959, however, considerable acreage was abandoned due to spring drought. The traditionally tight market in Nebraska was worse than ever, as custom cutters who had found little enough work to the south found none at all there. The next year Oklahoma had a good crop that gave custom cutters brief prosperity, but the usual surplus materialized in Nebraska.[10]

The story of custom combining through the 1950s was one of cyclical adjustment. Custom cutters responded rapidly to increased needs for their services, but only reluctantly to decreased demands, causing themselves occasional grief. Two classes of custom cutters evolved: professional harvesters and marginal operators. Professionals generally still were part-time farmers, but they at least made custom harvesting a regular feature of their annual routine. They cultivated customers for whom they harvested each year. Although poor markets and bad weather might reduce their business, they always had some wheat to cut. Marginal custom cutters were opportunists. When shortages of combines developed, they were ready to load up their machines and answer the call, especially if they had payments on their combines to meet. Often they gambled by making the harvest in years in which there was no special demand for their services, and usually they suffered for such audacity.

During the 1960s greater stability came to the business of custom cutting. The numbers of machines and men involved climbed to a higher plateau, noticeably in 1959 and 1960. This was not because of any return of prosperity to wheat farmers, but more likely because of the gradual effects of environment and the economy. More farmers came to regard custom combining as part of the natural order of affairs, rather than as a stopgap measure. The economies attendant to hiring custom cutters instead of owning combines were obvious, especially in the western reaches of the plains. Accordingly, the center of custom cutting gradually shifted west. Custom cutters also modified their routes in other ways. Wary of surpluses of combines that seemed always to develop in Nebraska, harvesters either rolled through to jobs in South Dakota or else turned around after their last stop in Kansas or Colorado.

During the 1960s governmental officials compiled few records about the activities of custom cutters. This was not because custom cutting was dying out, but because it became such an established institution that it no longer occasioned comment. By this time a new generation of custom cutters had grown up. In the Squires family of Taloga, Oklahoma, for instance, Everett's four sons worked in the harvest during the 1950s and 1960s, making the third generation of custom cutting Squires's. One of them, Richard, eventually would take over the business; Richard's two sons and daughter, then children growing up with the harvest, would compose a fourth generation of custom cutters.

No new outfits comparable to the Hammtowns of the early days were established during the 1950s and 1960s. Beginnings generally were humble and sometimes were simply matters of chance. In 1959 Russell Snell was wheat farming near Cherokee, Oklahoma, and had a new fourteen-foot Gleaner A combine that had cost him a little less than $5,000. A neighbor experienced in custom cutting urged Snell to make the harvest with him, and Snell agreed in order to get fuller use from his new machine. They harvested at home and for neighbors before pushing north to Dodge City and Smith Center in western Kansas and then into western Nebraska. Having a good year and liking the business, Snell continued in it until it was more important to him than his farming. When his friend quit in 1962, he bought a second combine, and in 1967 or 1968, a third. Snell eventually made his home in Ellinwood, Kansas, custom cutting in the summer and fall and suitcase farming his land near Cherokee.[11]

Another case was that of Jack Schlessiger from near Claflin, Kansas. From a farming family, he started casually in the business of custom cutting when his cousin in Hydrox, Oklahoma, sold him a combine in 1963. From there he custom cut his way home. He continued harvesting a short route on the southern plains with two combines for the next few years, but did not "get serious" about the business, he said, until 1966. That spring he advertised for jobs and traveled around to arrange work. Each year thereafter he took two or three machines from southern Oklahoma at least as far as western Nebraska and sometimes into the Dakotas or Montana. To Schlessiger, however, custom cutting remained a lesser activity related to a general farming operation with his father. Custom cutting enabled the Schlessigers to own better harvesting equipment than they could have otherwise, and profits from harvesting helped to stake purchases of additional land.[12]

Harvesters like Snell and Schlessiger were rewarded for their perseverance in the mid-1970s. From 1973 to 1976 bumper crops, coupled with high prices, created a doubly advantageous situation for wheat farmers and for custom cutters. High yields and expanded acreage, as farmers planted fencerow to fencerow, meant more work for harvesters and higher rates for doing it. Because farmers had ready cash, the price for harvesting rose for the first time since World War II, from about $3.00 an acre to about $8.00 an acre, with corresponding increases in charges for hauling and for heavy yields. Although during the same time the price of machinery and all other expenses incurred by custom cutters also increased rapidly, they were able to pass on these costs to their customers—painlessly, it seemed, in that time of prosperity. The rising price of machinery, combined with the flush times, helped to solidify the ranks of professional custom cutters. High price tags on new combines discouraged the sort of marginal operators who had entered the business during previous decades, and ensured that few farmers would purchase combines unless they were accustomed to do so. Most expansion in custom combining in the 1970s consisted of established operators increasing the size and quality of their outfits. Only a few new operators entered the field. Thus the new boom in custom cutting differed somewhat from earlier times of prosperity.

Custom cutting seemed like the greatest of occupations for a few years, but in the spring of 1977 custom harvesters were worried and financially embarrassed. The previous year cocky combiners had delighted in displaying their new combines, trucks, and trailers; in 1977 they crossed streets to avoid their bankers. Temporary prosperity had encouraged an excess of borrowing for machinery. When the price of wheat fell in the middle of 1976, custom cutters with heavy debts were as uncomfortable as were farmers with their wheat still in storage. Custom cutters feared that in 1977 farmers would balk at hiring harvesters to bring in grain that paid less than the cost of production. Instead, they might use the wheat for pasture or silage, or try to manage the harvest with what combines were available in the neighborhood. Drought threatened to take additional acres out of the harvest.

As the harvest unfolded, it proved not to be the fiasco feared. Along the Red River in Texas and Oklahoma there was

A Massey-Ferguson combine of the Ruben White outfit from Brownwood, Texas, cuts wheat in the North Canadian River valley west of Taloga, Oklahoma, 1977.

some cutting of prices, as farmers rebelled at paying $8.00 rates to cut $2.00 wheat, but this was an area where in previous years rates often had averaged lower than in other areas. As the harvest progressed through the southern plains, the rate for combining hung about where it had in 1976. Custom cutters with long-standing relationships with farmers found them sympathetic to pleas that increased expenses made lower rates impossible, although the farmers had no such ability to pass on costs to consumers. The weather also confused the situation, creating dislocations that bolstered the rate for cutting in certain areas. Heavy rains in Texas and Oklahoma bogged down many custom outfits, and some weeks later the same thing happened in southern Kansas.

Custom cutters of the 1970s were better able to weather hard times because they were less dependent on small grains

Grain trucks await their turns to dump at a country elevator west of Tribune, Kansas, 1977.

than were earlier operators. Custom cutters in the early years of the industry had only two choices if they wanted to extend their season into the fall: they could continue the spring wheat harvest through the northern parts of North Dakota and Montana into western Canada, or they could seek jobs cutting milo, usually near home. In parts of Texas, Oklahoma, Kansas, and Nebraska the milo harvest furnished profitable employment, but because harvesting milo was not the urgent sort of work that harvesting wheat was, it was hard for custom cutters to arrange many jobs for the fall.

Technological developments brought new opportunity to the fall harvest for custom cutters. Most important was the development of corn headers that converted grain combines into corn combines. Experiment stations and implement companies developed these corn headers on a practical basis in the early 1950s. Custom cutters thereafter could use their machines for corn as well as milo in the fall.[13]

The rapid expansion of groundwater irrigation on the plains in the 1960s created a whole new market for fall harvesters. Irrigation brought production of corn onto the high plains, the heart of custom cutting country. Custom cutters at first may have watched with dismay as regular customers replaced acreage in dryland wheat with fields of irrigated corn or milo, thinking that work would be lost, but they found that many farmers were willing to hire them for the fall harvest.

In addition, certain miscellaneous crops provided income for a few harvesters. By equipping headers with special pans to prevent losses from shattering, custom cutters could use their machines to harvest sunflowers. A few dozen custom cutters annually crossed La Veta Pass into the San Luis Valley of Colorado to pick up irrigated brewing barley. Occasionally, such jobs as threshing grass seed or alfalfa seed furnished profitable work.

Fall harvesting was one way that custom combining, rather than withering away as expected in the early years, adapted to become a perennial part of the agricultural economy of the Great Plains. Records retained by several state agencies revealed much of the character and extent of the modern business of custom combining. In the late 1960s the Bureau of Plant Industry of the Nebraska State Department of Agriculture recorded information about custom outfits entering the state from the south. The bureau's personnel collected the information while inspecting incoming combines for noxious weeds.[14]

The records showed that custom combining remained a flourishing business. In 1969 the bureau registered 1,897 custom outfits bringing in 4,250 combines. This was only about two-thirds the number of machines recorded by the state employment service for several years about a decade earlier, but the earlier registration program apparently was more complete than the later one. Also, considering the increase in size and efficiency of combines, the smaller number of machines registered in 1969 would have had the capacity to harvest more grain than the larger number a decade previous. Custom outfits came to Nebraska from roughly the same parts of the country as in earlier years (see Figure 5). Oklahoma and Kansas sent the largest delegations and, along with Texas, established the southern and central plains as the principal place of origin of custom cutters. North Dakota produced a sizeable group from the spring wheat region.

In 1976 the South Dakota Department of Public Safety also assembled a body of information about custom cutters, as that year for the first time the department issued special harvester's permits to custom cutters working in the state. The permits were available in each county seat. Probably few custom cutters working in the state escaped the count, but there were not as many harvesters as there would have been had it not been for severe drought in the west. Many outfits rolled right through the state to North Dakota or Montana without buying permits. Combines were not recorded on the permits, but 438 outfits were registered, using 815 trucks. They came from much the same states of origin as those in Nebraska, except that the states of the southern plains were relatively less important, North Dakota and Minnesota more so (see Figure 6). Far fewer custom combines were operating in the state than in the mid-1940s, but the drought largely explained the small number.[15]

The Montana Department of Highways used a similar system of permits in 1976. Six hundred and twenty-four outfits registered and brought 1,306 combines into the state, although drought also was prevalent in Montana. The custom cutters in the state came from the same general areas as those in the other states, except for relatively larger numbers from Oklahoma and Texas[16] (see Figure 7). About the same number of custom cutters and machines worked in North Dakota in 1976 as in Montana. The North Dakota Highway Department reported that it issued permits for 1,524 custom harvester's trucks in 1976, compared to 1,377 in 1975.[17]

The Economic Research Service of the United States Department of Agriculture, in cooperation with authorities in

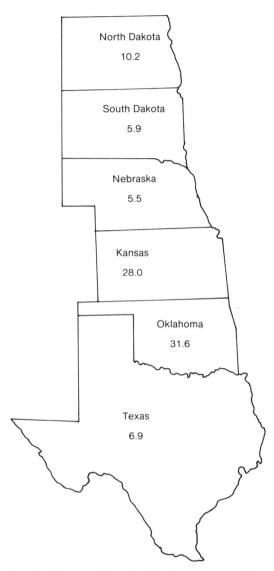

Fig. 5. Principal states of origin for custom combine outfits in Nebraska, 1969. Number in each state is percentage of outfits originating in the state. Data from Noxious Weeds Division, Bureau of Plant Industry, Nebraska State Department of Agriculture.

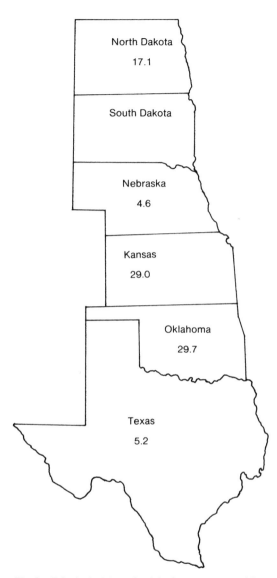

Fig. 6. Principal states of origin for custom combine outfits in South Dakota, 1976. Number in each state is the percentage of custom outfits originating in the state. Data from Division of Motor Vehicles, South Dakota Department of Public Safety.

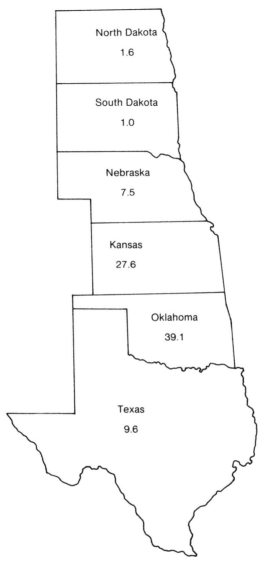

Fig. 7. Principal states of origin for custom combine outfits in Montana, 1976. Number in each state is the percentage of custom outfits originating in the state. Data from Montana Department of Highways.

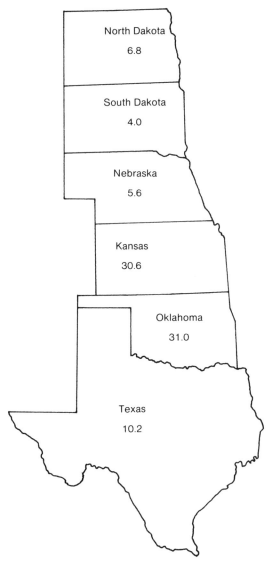

Fig. 8. Principal states of origin for custom combine outfits, 1971. Number in each state is the percentage of outfits originating in the state. Source: Lagrone and Gavett, *Interstate Custom Combining in the Great Plains in 1971.*

His work interrupted by light rain, custom cutter Chet Howe
watches while the combines empty their tanks into the truck.

the nine principal states in which custom cutters operated,
conducted the only comprehensive survey of the business of
custom combining in 1971.[18] This was before the sudden advent of prosperity for custom cutters in the 1970s. The au-
thors of the study did not reveal how many custom cutters
were named on their master list, compiled from lists submit-
ted from the nine states, but the number of respondents to
their survey was 3,431. In the harvest of 1971, these custom
cutters carried with them 7,551 combines, 7,946 grain trucks,
and 3,089 housing vehicles. They harvested 14.1 million acres
of crops, including 10.9 million acres of wheat, 32.4 percent of
the acreage in wheat in the nine states covered. Also included
were 1.3 million acres of grain sorghum, 173,000 acres of soybeans, and 732,000 acres of other crops (corn among these,

but not specified). Although custom cutters came from as far away as both coasts—from California and Florida—most came from the traditional places of origin for custom cutters (see Figure 8). Oklahoma and Kansas led the field by far as states of origin, followed by Texas and North Dakota. How much grain was harvested by custom cutters not reached by the survey or not responding to it was impossible to tell. The results obtained were enough to show the continuation and the importance of custom combining in the Great Plains.

Custom combining had outlasted its early critics and detractors. Rather than destroying the business, hard times and economic adjustments had thinned and hardened the ranks of the participants. To both custom cutters and farmers, the industry had become an established institution not to be discarded lightly.

Chapter 4
Custom Combining in the
Agriculture of the Great Plains

Custom combining originated in response to difficult circumstances associated with World War II, but in ensuing years the industry established a permanent niche in the agricultural economy of the plains. Custom cutting was a hazardous, unpredictable business, for each cruel cycle of the agricultural economy affected it. Moreover, custom cutting was based on the most hectic and anguishing aspect of farming, the harvest. Yet the business showed remarkable tenacity. Professional custom combiners rode out hard times and refused to quit.

The business survived because these entrepreneurs of the harvest filled the particular needs of farmers on the plains. They also achieved their own goals, generally the ambitions of frustrated farmers seeking outlets for initiative and capital. After the first few years of the business, custom cutting was free enterprise in an almost pure sense, with all attendant problems and benefits. Without effective central direction, there was no preventing temporary difficulties when contraction followed expansion. Even in the midst of agricultural conditions so often swayed by fluctuations of the economy, actions of the government, and conditions of the weather, custom cutters imposed on the harvest measures of order, efficiency, and flexibility. They accomplished this incidentally, as each individual operator attempted to stabilize his own business.

When a farmer hired a custom cutter, he paid his money for three commodities—machinery, labor, and expertise. The

Crewmen of the Ruben White outfit work to clear a plugged cylinder that stopped their work in Oklahoma, 1977.

combine was an investment both expensive and seasonal. The intricacies of its mechanisms and the bulk of its materials made the combine the most costly machine a farmer might own, but it was used only for the few frenetic weeks of harvest and stood idle the rest of the year. If stored outside, it depreciated rapidly; if kept inside, it took up shed space. For many farmers the combine was a mechanical elephant not worth the expense of keeping. They preferred to hire custom cutters, who put machinery to use throughout the summer and fall.

Farmers also found it difficult to recruit the laborers they needed for harvest, because the work was of short duration. Before the coming of the combine, unskilled migrant workers filled out harvest and threshing crews, working under the watchful eyes of farmers and threshermen. Harvesting with combines, however, required men with certain skills beyond those of an educated pitchfork. Workers not only had to be able to drive combines and trucks, but also had to understand their operation enough to do maintenance and make adjustments. A few men knowledgeable about such work moved unattached with the harvest each year, as had the bindlestiffs before them, but farmers hated to depend on them. Custom cutters hired workers for the entire harvest season, and if some were green at the start of the year, they soon learned the skills they needed. Custom cutters relieved farmers of the problem of assembling experienced help.

Finally, custom cutters brought specialized knowledge to their task. Farmers harvested only a few weeks of the year and spent the rest of their time at other pursuits. They were skilled in many jobs, but spent too little time at the wheel to become experts in the operation of combines. Custom cutters made their living by harvesting. They knew more about combines than anyone else. Although farmers sometimes wondered whether custom cutters saved other people's grain as carefully as they might their own, they acknowledged the ability of custom cutters to do good work when they were so inclined.

Employment of custom cutters appealed to certain classes of farmers more than to others. Custom harvesters agreed that their customers fell into two rough classes, big farmers and small farmers, exact limits undefined. Farmers with only small acreage, perhaps a quarter or half section, employed custom cutters because combines were inordinate investments for them. Part-time farmers especially favored custom cutters because their other work prevented them from supplying the concentrated effort required for the harvest. The same was true for farmers on the verge of retirement. On the eastern edge of the area of operations for custom cutters, there were many small landholdings belonging to people who had no choice but to hire custom cutters.

Farmers operating large acreages hired custom cutters more from choice than from necessity. Big farmers found that

The Bernel Elmore outfit from Shattuck, Oklahoma, operated fifteen combines on its larger jobs in 1977, and traffic got heavy when the machines came to the trucks to dump.

harvesting their crops required enormous amounts of capital and troublesome dealings with labor. It also taxed their skills of management. Big farmers, therefore, chose to employ custom cutters' package offers of machinery, labor, and expertise.

Farmers with acreages falling in the middle range tended to do more of their own harvesting. They had enough use to justify owning combines, but not so much that they could not find and manage sufficient help for harvest.

These trends in hiring custom cutters began early in the history of the business, as was shown in a study of custom harvesting in Oklahoma in 1948. A survey of a limited sample of wheat farmers, seventy of them, found thirty-seven who owned no combines. Nearly all of these owned fewer than 300 acres of wheat, and nearly half owned fewer than 100 acres. These farmers obviously had no choice but to hire custom cutters, except for harvesting a bit of oats and barley with binders. Thirty-three of the farmers surveyed owned their own combines, but of these, many still hired custom cutters. The thirteen farmers with combines who each had fewer than 100 acres of wheat hired about a third of their wheat cut; the sixteen who each had between 100 and 300 acres, about a fifth; the four who each had more than 300 acres, about two-fifths.

With the price of wheat sliding in 1948, nearly all farmers polled indicated that they intended to cut back on hiring custom cutters in the future. Even many farmers who owned no combines indicated they would stop hiring harvesters and presumably buy their own machines. Farmers in general did not curtail hiring custom cutters in succeeding years as much as the farmers in this sample indicated, for had they done so, custom combining would have shrunk into insignificance.[1]

The survey happened to catch the farmers at a time when they were frustrated and angry about the uncertain market for wheat. They did not see how they could afford to hire custom cutters in the future, for they still regarded custom combining as a temporary expedient and a rather extravagant one. Few yet had paused to consider that, in the long run, custom harvesting might be the most economical method for many farmers.

Farmers, especially small farmers, also were dissatisfied with the service provided by custom cutters in 1948. More than one-third of the farmers with fewer than 100 acres of wheat reported that custom combiners from outside the area did poor work, apparently meaning that they did an inadequate job of saving grain. Smaller numbers of larger farmers agreed. About the same proportion of small farmers said that custom cutters failed to "clean up the area," or finish all the wheat in the area before moving out, and larger farmers tended to agree. Other complaints were that custom cutters abandoned farmers before all the work on the farm was done, refused to cut fields isolated by distance from other work, or delayed harvest because they were late in arriving in the area. All classes of farmers agreed to some extent with these contentions. More important, however, was that in none of these complaints did the majority of farmers concur, indicating that custom combining as a system was working satisfactorily, but that certain farmers had suffered bad experiences.[2]

Complaints about poor work voiced by small farmers were explainable on two counts. First, custom cutters could not have been expected to be as conscientious about harvesting for small farmers as for big ones. Some custom cutters might not care if they left a farmer of eighty acres unhappy with their work, for the job was too minor to worry about. A farmer with 500 acres of wheat, however, was a customer to be cultivated carefully. Small farmers complained more vocally, also, because they felt helpless. Since fewer of them owned combines, they were utterly dependent on custom cutters. If a small farmer had the misfortune to hire a custom cutter who did poor work, he had little recourse. If he ran the shoddy harvesters off his place, then the word went around that he was too picky to work for, and the farmer was likely to end up with no one to cut his wheat.

Although the quality of work done by custom cutters improved greatly in succeeding years, the same sort of complaints survived, especially among small farmers. Small farmers continued to be the most critical of custom cutters' work, always with some justification. Because of this, many farmers chose to buy their own combines in spite of the savings of hiring custom cutters. They felt more secure having their own machines, even if they were old and decrepit ones.

Not only the size of farms but also the type of farming operations determined whether farmers found it practical to hire custom cutters. The less the diversification in crops on a farm, the greater the need for custom cutters. Farmers who raised only wheat had short harvesting seasons and got only limited use from combines they owned themselves. They did better to hire custom cutters, regardless of how many acres they farmed. Farmers who had several different crops had more extended periods of harvest. They might use their combines first for small grains and later for other crops.

Geography dictated many of the farming practices that in

turn affected custom cutting. In the northern plains farmers often grew a variety of spring crops—wheat, durum wheat, barley, oats, and rye—each of them ripening at a slightly different time. By planning the time for windrowing the differing crops, farmers could stretch out their season for combining small grains. In the southern plains there was less diversification in small grains, and because wheat was seeded in the fall, the grain ripened evenly and the harvest had to be done as quickly as possible. Extending use of the combine on the southern plains depended on the possibility of raising some crop harvested in the fall, such as corn, milo, or soybeans.

There were other areas in which farming practices had special effect. In places where both spring wheat and winter wheat were grown, such as South Dakota, farmers could prolong the use of their combines, for the winter wheat ripened before the spring wheat. This made it more practical to own combines on the farm. The opposite effect was present in areas of the southern plains where farmers raised both cotton and winter wheat, such as northwest Texas. There, if farmers wanted to own all their own harvesting machinery, they had to buy two complete sets—grain combines and cotton pickers. Therefore, it was practical for many to rely on custom cutters to harvest the wheat.

In many smaller localities, unusual conditions stimulated or limited the activities of custom cutters. The practice of terracing made custom cutting more difficult, for combining on terraced fields had to be done in contour with the terraces instead of in circular patterns. Location of highways also had an effect. Custom cutters were most numerous along major highways running north and south. They were less willing to unload and work on a small job if it was located some distance from the main highway than if it was right on their route.

Custom combining was more common in the western parts of the wheat belt of the Great Plains than on the eastern fringe. Farming on the high plains was characterized by large acreages and little diversification, unless groundwater for irrigation was available. The big farmers of this area raised so little of any other crop besides winter wheat that they could use

77

Combines from the Clair and Chet Howe outfit cut long rows of wheat between strips of fallow near Torrington, Wyoming, in 1978.

combines only for a short season. Inconsistent rainfall caused frequent crop failures. In a year of drought, farmers with their own combines had valuable machinery standing idle. The suitcase farmers so numerous in areas such as western Kansas and eastern Colorado, who lived in towns distant from their lands, had particular need for dependable harvesters whom they could hire and set to work with little supervision. The coming of irrigation changed all this in some places, as irrigated crops replaced dryland wheat and reduced the summer's business for custom cutters. Yet because of convenience or because of habit from earlier times, many farmers practicing irrigation continued to hire custom cutters, not only for their wheat, but also for fall harvest of corn or milo.

Counts of custom cutters inspected at ports of entry along

the southern border of Nebraska illustrated the tendency for custom combining to settle upon the high plains. This already was evident in 1942 and 1947, when inspectors found the largest numbers of machines entering the state through southwestern ports of entry (see Figure 1, Chapter 2). Totals reported by Nebraska's weed inspectors two decades later, in 1969, confirmed that the earlier trend for custom cutting to find its home on the high plains had continued. Most outfits entered the state in the southwest, particularly at Benkelman and McCook (see Figure 9).[3]

Figures from the federal agricultural census of 1974 also indicated the western orientation of custom cutting. Census enumerators recorded farmers' expenses not for custom combining in particular, but for custom work in general. In areas of winter wheat farming, most expense for custom work would have been for custom combining. Moreover, farmers would have employed other types of custom operators for much the same reasons that they employed custom combiners. An area of custom work in a region of winter wheat farming such as Kansas was presumably an area of custom combining. (This was not necessarily so in regions where other crops encouraged different types of custom work, as did cotton in Texas and southern Oklahoma.)

The amount of custom work per cultivated acre was much higher in the western counties of Kansas than in the eastern counties, showing the prevalence of custom combining in the west (see Figure 10). With certain exceptions, such as the sand hills of the far southwest, the custom combining belt in Kansas in 1974 stretched from the south-central region across the western parts of the state, the amount of custom work declining to the east. A similar investigation for Oklahoma showed that custom work was common in the northwest part of that state, a region adjacent to the area of custom cutting in south-central Kansas. In Nebraska custom work was most evident in the southwestern part of the state and in the Panhandle.[4]

Statistics compiled by the Kansas Crop and Livestock Reporting Service in 1976 showed the same general trends as

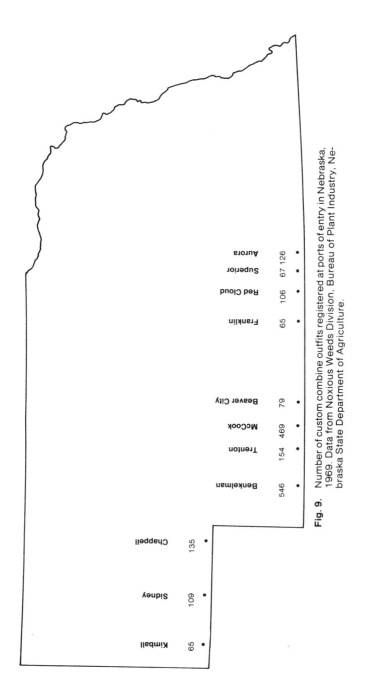

Fig. 9. Number of custom combine outfits registered at ports of entry in Nebraska, 1969. Data from Noxious Weeds Division, Bureau of Plant Industry, Nebraska State Department of Agriculture.

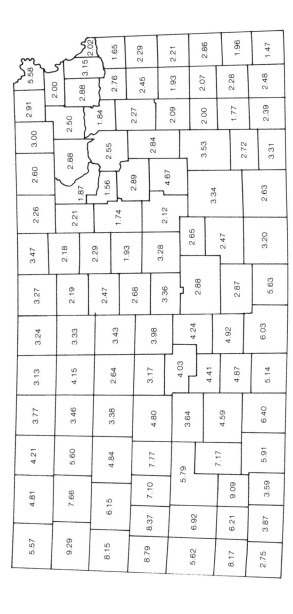

Fig. 10. Dollars per cultivated acre spent by farmers in Kansas for custom work in 1974. Compiled from United States Census of Agriculture, 1974.

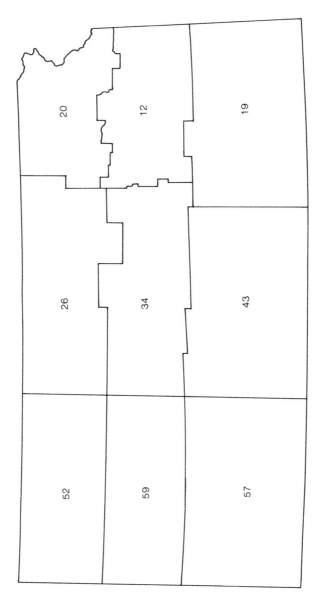

Fig. 11. Percentage of acres of wheat custom cut in the nine crop-and-livestock reporting districts of Kansas, 1976. Data from Kansas Crop and Livestock Reporting Service.

had the census of 1974. The Crop and Livestock Reporting Service computed the percentage of wheat custom cut in each of nine crop and livestock reporting districts in Kansas, as reported by county extension agents. The results confirmed that the area of custom combining embraced the south-central and western parts of the state (see Figure 11). The importance of custom harvesting was most obvious in the western one-third of the state, where more than one-half of the wheat was custom cut.[5]

In 1964 the Statistical Reporting Service of the United States Department of Agriculture had compiled information on the extent of custom combining in nine states of the Great Plains. The results, although they showed the percentage of wheat and other crops custom combined only for whole states, indicated both the predominance of custom cutting in the west and the strength of the business on the southern plains, as opposed to the northern plains (see Table 4). Texas and Oklahoma had the greatest percentage of wheat harvested by custom work, but, considering the great acreage of wheat in Kansas, that state furnished more custom work in the wheat harvest than any other. The winter wheat states of the southern and central plains—Texas, Oklahoma, Kansas, Colorado, and Nebraska—all hosted much custom work in the wheat harvest. So did South Dakota, but North Dakota and Montana showed smaller percentages of custom work. Similar trends emerged for combining other grains, which included oats, barley, rice, flax, and milo. Texas, with its great acreage of other grains and its high percentage of them custom combined, was outstanding in this category. This reflected the large amount of custom milo harvesting done by crews from within the state during the summer.[6]

Reports as to where custom cutting was most common showed not only the preferences of farmers but also the settings in which custom cutters developed their harvesting itineraries, or routes, as they generally called them. In choosing where to work, custom cutters weighed the demand for their services in various areas, but they also were governed by other considerations. Most custom cutters were part-time

Table 4.

Percentage of Wheat and Other Grains Custom Combined, 1964

State	Wheat		Other Grains	
	Thousands of Acres Combined	% Custom Combined	Thousands of Acres Combined	% Custom Combined
Texas	3,017	42	6,526	35
Oklahoma	4,201	40	1,440	33
Kansas	9,576	29	3,934	23
Colorado	1,707	35	699	35
Nebraska	2,953	32	3,059	26
South Dakota	2,139	35	3,615	25
Wyoming	224	24	210	26
North Dakota	6,236	21	6,842	15
Montana	3,724	22	1,828	25

Source: Statistical Bulletin 377, Statistical Reporting Service, United States Department of Agriculture.

farmers, and so one point on each harvester's route had to be the home place, to harvest his own wheat. Custom cutters also tended to follow the line of least resistance along the best highways running north and south, sometimes thereby overlooking available work isolated from main lines of travel.

In other respects the route of each custom cutter developed according to a series of chance events. Many beginning custom cutters were fortunate enough to start in the business in partnership with an experienced harvester who already had jobs arranged. Otherwise, the novice headed for the vicinity of the Red River in May and moved from there to wherever he heard, or hoped, there was work available. Each time he found work, he tried to make an agreement with the farmer he cut for to come back and cut again the next year. In this manner, unless he went broke first, the custom cutter built his route, with much variation in it for the first few years.

Once custom cutters had established regular routes, they generally were reluctant to change them, but in any particular year one or more stops on a route might be wiped out by drought, hail, or some other disaster. In such cases custom cutters tried to find work to carry them over until they were needed at the next stop. This often meant trying another area, perhaps meeting a new customer, and then establishing a new stop on the route to replace the old one, not just for the single year, but also thereafter.

In other instances custom cutters modified their routes because of deliberate decisions of management. Most custom cutters fell into one of two schools of thought: some were proponents of a western route, sometimes called the duster's route, while others were adherents of an eastern route, or the mudder's route. There were advantages and disadvantages to either approach. Custom cutters who kept to the high plains of the western route maintained that the way to make the most money was to cover the most acres, even if yields were poor. Farmers on the high plains offered jobs big enough to keep outfits busy without causing too much wasted time moving from place to place. Seldom was harvest delayed by rain or mud in the west. Even the dew was light, and so crews could work late into the night and start early in the morning without the wheat becoming too tough. The disadvantages of a western route were frequent crop failures and generally low yields.

Farther east yields consistently were higher, meaning greater revenues from charges for hauling and for high yields. Crop failures were rare, and when they came, they usually resulted from a local condition, such as hail. The eastern route was more stable than the western route. The disadvantage was the greater frequency of rain. Too often custom cutters found themselves unable to work because of wet wheat and muddy fields. Such idleness meant that outfits were delayed in reaching their next stops. Heavy dew also forced custom cutters to quit work soon after nightfall and to wait at least until midmorning to begin.

The debate over western and eastern routes was only partly

a result of conscious choices by custom cutters. More important in determining routes were the harvesters' places of origin. Custom cutters from Texas, for instance, tended to stay to the west. Starting from their homes and moving north by the most direct routes, they traveled through western Oklahoma, the Texas Panhandle, western Kansas, eastern Colorado, and western Nebraska. If they went farther north, they generally headed for Montana rather than North Dakota. Custom cutters from central Oklahoma or central Kansas, on the other hand, tended to move straight north from their homes. This eventually took them into the Dakotas.

Partial shifts in route were common, nevertheless. Custom cutters who experienced several muddy years in central Kansas sometimes vowed to find a better way, and the next year found them in parts west. Others became disillusioned with work in North Dakota, maybe because of rain, perhaps because of the scarcity of work, or even just because they were tired of hauling pickup headers to use there. Montana beckoned to them with its dry climate and its straight-cutting. So it was common for custom cutters to travel both north and west with the harvest. This was made easy by the later ripening of wheat at higher western altitudes. Custom cutters could cut their way into central Kansas, for instance, and then switch tracks westward, making another stop in northeastern Colorado. Others might cut through South Dakota and then leap to Montana.

Planning harvesting routes involved more than merely deciding on general areas in which to operate. It also meant arranging specific stops on the route at proper intervals. In this the custom cutter had to act judiciously: stops had to be far enough apart that there was sufficient time to finish one job before the next was ready, but close enough that there was little idle time between them. If stops on the route were close together, then the acreage cut at each had to be small. Custom cutters always hoped to develop routes with fewer stops and more acres at each stop. Small jobs were culled from the itinerary if additional work became available at major stops on the route.

Custom cutters also changed their routes gradually because of changes in practices by farmers. Sometimes custom cutters found that routes that had seemed well arranged for many years became unmanageable. Looking over records of previous years, they discovered that the dates of harvest had changed, because farmers had begun planting varieties of wheat that matured earlier. Such dislocations occasionally forced custom cutters to break ties with farmers for whom they had harvested for decades. Other changes might be more sudden and obvious: increased summer fallowing meant less acreage of wheat; increased irrigation meant less wheat but more fall harvesting.

As fall approached each year, attrition thinned the ranks of combiners working the wheat harvest. Part-time farmers from the southern plains returned home to put seed in the ground and children in school. Hired hands went off to high school or college. A hard core of combiners continued north with the wheat harvest into the northernmost parts of North Dakota or Montana, a few even moving into the prairie provinces of Canada. Along with wheat, there might be flax to pick up or sunflowers to combine.

Custom cutters who returned south did not necessarily quit custom cutting for the year. Most also made a fall harvest of corn or milo, usually in the areas of their own homes. The departure of custom cutters from the small grain harvest late in the year was not so much the end of the season for those leaving as merely a divergence in harvesting routes, some going on north, others back south.

The length of the harvesting season varied greatly among custom cutters. Larger outfits generally worked longer seasons than smaller ones. In 1971 the average length of season for outfits with one combine was 89 days; the average for outfits with two machines was 119 days; the average for outfits with three combines was 125 days; the averages for outfits with more than three combines were about 150 days. These figures included both the small grain harvest and the fall harvest.[7]

Although some outfits made as many as ten or eleven stops

in the small grain harvest, seven or eight stops were considered a full season. A few custom cutters, mostly from the southern plains, made only three or four stops. Often the last stop on the route, if it was in North Dakota or Montana, had the most acres. According to information about the harvest of 1977 supplied by thirty-two custom cutters, larger outfits made longer runs and made more stops in the small grain harvest than did smaller ones. Outfits with only two combines generally made five or six stops, while outfits with three or more machines usually made seven or more.[8]

Each stop on the route was made up of one or more specific jobs with farmers. Obtaining such jobs was a process usually unsystematic and often puzzling. After the early years of the business, when to meet the needs of wartime the government exercised some direction of custom cutters, harvesters generally eschewed governmental placement services. When custom cutters entered an unfamiliar town they parked in some place that harvesters were known to frequent, so that farmers would be able to find them. Then the custom cutters began asking around for work, probably visiting the county employment office and the county agent's office, but placing just as much confidence in restaurants, pool halls, elevator offices, and implement dealerships. In this manner they often got leads as to which farmers needed harvesters. If not, and if they were ambitious, they began driving country roads looking for ripe wheat without any combines sitting around the farmyard. Stopping at each likely place, they inquired if the farmers needed combiners or knew of anyone who did.

At other times the situation was reversed, and it was farmers who sought harvesters. Then the farmers drove into town and looked for combines parked in the usual places, probably finding several outfits. From among them they made their choices of whom to approach with offers for work, acting on various criteria, some obvious and others unexplainable. Curious, they examined the prospects. Some farmers seemed to choose by color: John Deere was a good brand, one might think, and so he looked for green, while others sought the crimson of Massey-Harris (Massey-Ferguson) or the silver of

Gleaner-Baldwin (Allis-Chalmers Gleaner). Farmers looked over machinery to see if it was new and clean, examined license tags to see where the outfit was from, and scrutinized crewmen to decide if they looked respectable. If a farmer liked what he saw, he approached the boss with the casual question, "You looking for cutting?"—and a bargain was struck.

Such scenarios became scarcer with each passing year. Not only did custom cutters usually retain the same lots of customers year after year, but when they altered their arrangements, they tried to pass their customers on to friends. If a custom cutter had to abandon cutting for a particular farmer, he considered whether he had a fellow harvester who might appreciate the business, and his recommendation usually resulted in a satisfactory arrangement.

Some custom cutters advertised for work. This was done best in agricultural periodicals, most notably in the *High Plains Journal* of Dodge City, Kansas, the closest thing to a marketplace in print for custom cutters. In classified advertisements under the heading, "Harvesting," custom cutters stated in what parts of the country they needed work. Occasionally custom cutters getting out of the business after some years of experience advertised to sell "established operations." This meant that buyers purchased lists of steady customers along with the outfits' machinery.

Perhaps the most fascinating aspect of custom combining as a business was that such an important institution was held together by informal, verbal agreements. Written contracts between farmers and custom cutters were so rare as to be insignificant. If a custom cutter harvested for a farmer one year, it generally was understood that he would come back for the same job the next year, unless one of the parties had reason to be dissatisfied. An affirmative answer to the farmer's query, "Be back next year?" constituted an agreement. Also understood was that either party might have to back out of the arrangement if circumstances dictated. The farmer might lose his crop to hail and be unable to offer any cutting. The custom cutter might be delayed by rain at an earlier stop. This posed an awkward situation. If the custom cutter left the job he was on in order to meet his commitment farther north, then the farmer he left behind would be embittered. If he stayed to finish the job he was on, then the next customer down the line grew anxious.

The only way to avoid hard feelings was through constant communication. This started long before harvest began. Custom combiners corresponded with their customers intermittently through the winter, affirming oral agreements but not formalizing them, asking how the wheat was doing and how many acres there would be to cut. Christmas cards were a handy excuse for such inquiries. Letters proliferated as spring progressed, as custom cutters preparing to leave for Texas tried to plan a definite route for the season. A few visited each prospective customer in the spring. This annual ritual of making the rounds was a sure way of cultivating steady customers.

As harvest began, custom cutters arranged for their customers to reach them by telephone wherever they were. If someone in the harvester's family stayed at home during harvest, then the home folks formed a control center for the outfit, taking messages from customers and keeping them informed as to where the outfit was. Otherwise, the custom cutter gave each customer a list of telephone numbers where he could be reached at his various stops. Custom cutters seldom waited for farmers to call them during harvest, but ran up their own telephone bills in order to stay in touch.

If a custom cutter was unable to arrive at a job when the wheat was ready, usually because of rain and mud, he informed the farmer concerned. If the relationship between the two was long-standing, then the farmer was willing to wait a couple of days, but probably not more than that. When the farmer decided he could wait no longer, he sought someone else for the job. He was expected to notify the custom cutter of this and generally did so.

At other times the custom cutter took the initiative in suspending an agreement. He might inform the customer he was working for that he could delay there no longer and had to move on to his next job. This almost always caused hard feel-

A thunderstorm of rain and dust threatens to interrupt the work of the Bernel Elmore outfit near Watkins, Colorado, in 1978.

ings, and so the custom cutter tried to find some other harvester to finish the work if possible. As an alternative, the custom cutter might call ahead and tell the next customer on his itinerary to go ahead and hire another cutter. He made the decision as to whom to break an arrangement with on the basis of which job had the most acres to cut and which customer he had worked for the longest. A custom cutter with four or more combines had an advantage in situations like this. He could send a respectable outfit of two machines ahead to his next job and leave two to clean up in the mud.

Some of the largest outfits planned their routes with the idea of splitting up to work in two or more parties most of the time. The separate contingents either could leapfrog past each other from stop to stop, or they could move parallel to each other on a series of jobs, coming together only for the biggest ones. The outfit of Bernel Elmore of Shattuck, Oklahoma, perhaps the largest outfit in the field in 1977, with fifteen John Deere combines, split into two contingents for most of the season. All the machines were together only at the beginning of the season in Texas and later in Colorado and Montana.

The system of verbal agreements held together remarkably well. It was reliable enough that farmers trusted it and custom cutters planned on it, and yet flexible enough to allow for adjustments due to unforeseen circumstances. Sometimes individual farmers or custom cutters acted irresponsibly, and such actions left a bitter taste. "When we were first starting out," recalled one custom cutting wife, "I remember my husband calling ahead for a job of cutting for a farmer. He kept in touch for at least a month, then after traveling 6 or 8 hours getting there, with our trucks and machines, we found another crew in the yard. The farmer then proceeded to bargain for who would cut the cheapest." She added, "We left immediately and have not returned to that area."[9] Such occurrences were memorable because they were out of the ordinary.

Both economic self-interest and personal honor worked to enforce the discipline of informal contracts. The unwritten code of custom combining was a flexible one, but the person who stretched it beyond reason suffered the consequences. The custom cutter who failed to live up to his obligations to a farmer found it hard to obtain work in the locality the next year. Likewise, if a farmer reneged on an agreement, the word spread among custom cutters working the area, and the farmer might be left with no harvesters at all. Most farmers found it best to hire the same cutters each year and to pay them the going rate for harvesting. Perennial dependability was more important than possibly saving a half-dollar to the acre in rates, money that might be lost anyway to careless threshing by an unfamiliar cutter.

The manner of quoting the going rate, or charge for cutting

Hauling charges were less if the custom crew trucked the grain only as far as bins on the farm, as was the case for the Richard Squires outfit on the Ken Prosser farm near Towner, Colorado, in 1977.

small grains, became standardized early in the history of custom combining. Custom cutters charged a set fee for each acre combined, whether the grain was straight-cut as it stood or picked up from the windrow. Added to this base rate was a charge for each bushel hauled to storage. There was an extra charge for combining fields with high yields, a specified number of cents for each bushel to the acre more than twenty. The price for combining an acre was expressed in dollars, the price for hauling in cents, and the price for high yields also in cents, the three numbers being quoted together in the parlance of the harvest. A charge of "eight, ten, and ten" meant that the custom cutter received $8.00 an acre as a base rate, ten cents a bushel for hauling, and ten cents for every bushel of yield more than twenty bushels to the acre.

Amendments to this formula adapted it to special situations. Hauling charges included an escalator if the distance to the elevator was too far. This meant that added to the usual rate for hauling there was an extra charge on each bushel for every mile more than five miles that it was hauled. If the rate for hauling was ten cents, and an escalator of one cent was added, then the cost of hauling a bushel ten miles to an elevator was fifteen cents. If wheat was to be hauled only as far as a bin on the farm, then the charge for hauling was lessened. In such a case the custom cutter might even relinquish all charges for hauling and negotiate a flat rate for combining and hauling to the bin, which would be expressed by a phrase like "nine dollars in the bin."

In some other cases, it was obvious that the yield from a field would be low, for instance, in a field damaged by drought or hail. The custom cutter and the farmer then might agree on a simple, low flat rate to salvage the little grain left standing. The situation might be quite different. Perhaps a combination of rank growth and untimely rains caused good wheat to lodge. Then the custom cutter might demand extra compensation for the slow work necessary to save grain lying close to the ground. In any situation the custom cutter might alter the formula of his rates to fit personal preferences or special crops. Custom cutters often discriminated in favor of large customers, waiving certain charges in order to obtain their business. Some farmers preferred to pay for combining from the windrow by the bushel rather than by the acre. Combining malt barley for brewing, for instance, was a special case. The grain had to be threshed carefully, sometimes under the eyes of supervisors from the brewery, to avoid cracking, which spoiled the barley for brewing. The payment for such work was by the bushel.

The going rate for combining in any year was the result of a free market, but did not necessarily reflect perfectly the relationship of supply and demand. The demand for custom work depended on the acreage to be harvested, the yield of the crop, and the ability of farmers to pay for harvesting. When the market for wheat was strong, farmers planted more acres and were better able to pay for harvesting. Rates then rose rapidly. When the market for wheat declined, then farmers planted fewer acres and had less cash to pay for harvesting. At such times, however, there was no sudden decline in the going rate for cutting. Instead, the rate remained about the same, and the collapse in the market was reflected in less work available. In good times custom cutters reaped quick profits on high charges that farmers regarded as painless at the time. In hard times rates seldom declined, but locked into archaic schedules with no allowance for steadily increasing expenses.

Prices also varied a bit from region to region in any one year. As harvest began along the Red River, a surplus of combines usually arrived before the wheat was ready, and so rates for cutting in northern Texas and southern Oklahoma often were slightly lower than those farther north. As the harvest entered full swing in central Oklahoma and southern Kansas, the going rate prevailed unless there was some special circumstance. The price sometimes dipped again in Nebraska because of the chronic surpluses of combines there. The going rate then ruled on north to the Canadian border. In Canada the rate often was lower than in the United States.

Rates received during the early 1940s were excellent for the times. The going rate from 1942 through 1947 was three-fifty, five, and five, meaning $3.50 an acre base rate, five cents a bushel for hauling, and five cents a bushel for each bushel per acre more than twenty. Base rates of $3.00 or $4.00 an acre also were common. Usually there was a charge of a half-cent per bushel per mile for hauling wheat more than five miles. As the harvest began each year in Texas, base rates generally were lower, about $2.50 an acre.[10]

These rates did not collapse with the coming of hard times after 1948. For more than two decades thereafter, rates stayed about the same, fluctuating only occasionally with temporary circumstances. The going rate constituted a floor below which rates rarely dipped, but custom cutters were unable to pass on increased costs or compensate for inflation.

Intermittent records of rates kept by various state agencies confirmed the recollections of custom cutters about these difficult years for the industry. From 1948 through 1953 the North Dakota State Employment Service reported prevailing rates of three-fifty, five, and five or four, five, and five each year. An average base rate of $2.31 an acre reported for Alberta in 1950 showed the lower trend there. The Nebraska Crop and Livestock Reporting Service recorded custom rates for certain years in the 1950s and 1960s, but failed to note the rates by the formula that custom cutters used. The only trend plain from the compilation was that the base rate held about even at $3.50 or $4.00.[11]

Relief from low rates started in 1973 and continued during the next few years. From 1974 through 1976 rates of eight, ten, and ten were common. The rising trend was evident in rates reported by the Kansas Crop and Livestock Reporting Service in a number of years (see Table 5). A report for Texas in 1973 showed that the increase in rates that year began there, but that prices never reached the levels of the going rate farther north the same year. The base rate most frequently charged there was $4.00, and the average was about the same. The charge for trucking rose to ten or fifteen cents, but the charge for high yields remained a nickel. Returns from South Dakota in 1970 and 1975 reflected a rise in the going rate from three-fifty, five, and five to eight, ten, and ten. Rates in Canada also rose, but lagged behind those in the United States. The Saskatchewan Department of Agriculture recommended a base rate of $7.00 in 1975 and $8.00 in 1976, and the Canadian dollar suffered slightly in the exchange for United States currency.[12]

Rates for harvesting other small grains were about the same as for wheat. On the southern plains, where combining oats or barley was unusual work, rates for these crops ran a few cents higher than rates for wheat. In the Dakotas, where more oats, barley, and rye were grown, rates for these small grains ran slightly less than those for wheat.

Table 5.

Rates for Custom Wheat Harvesting in Kansas, 1961–76

Year	Average Base Rate per Acre for Combining	Average Charge per Bushel for Hauling	Average Charge per Bushel for High Yields
1961	$3.65	$ .05	$ .05
1965	3.52	.05	.05
1970	3.76	.05	.05
1973	4.83	.05	.05
1974	8.09	.09	.09
1975	8.45	.09	.09
1976	8.66	.09	.09

Source: Reports on Custom Rates by Kansas Crop and Livestock Reporting Service.

Custom cutters adapted the formula by which they charged for combining small grains and applied it also to milo. The only difference in principle was that the charge for high yields applied to every bushel more than thirty or forty to the acre rather than twenty. The base rate per acre for combining milo averaged higher than that for cutting wheat. In 1961 in Kansas, for instance, the average base rate for milo was $3.80, fifteen cents above that for wheat. The margin spread a few cents each year, until, by 1975, the average base rate for milo, $9.28, was eighty-three cents higher than that for wheat. The rise in the price for milo harvesting, however, occurred at the same time as that for wheat. Charges for hauling and for high yields were about the same per bushel for milo as for wheat. Because yields for milo were higher than those for wheat, the total charges accumulated for hauling were much higher.[13]

Charges for combining corn sometimes were computed on a different basis. The usual practice in areas growing dryland corn, such as eastern Kansas, was to charge a base rate for each acre and an additional charge for each bushel combined. This was economic recognition that in corn harvesting, high

97

yields were as much a factor in the difficulty of a job as was acreage. Rates for combining corn by this formula moved upward parallel to those for wheat. The Kansas Crop and Livestock Reporting Service first reported rates for combining corn in 1970, recording an average rate of $5.65 an acre plus four cents a bushel. In six years these charges about doubled. In 1976 the average reported rates were $12.13 an acre plus eight cents a bushel. Added to these prices were hauling charges at levels about the same as those for wheat. Where irrigated corn was grown, such as in western Kansas, prices were figured by a different formula. Hauling charges were much the same, but the base rate for cutting was expressed in a rate per bushel, the number of acres being irrelevant when yields were as high as they were under irrigation. From 1970 to 1976, the rate for this sort of work advanced from ten cents a bushel to nineteen cents a bushel. In some cases charges for cutting irrigated milo also were figured by the bushel.[14]

Rates charged for custom combining were part of the relationship between custom cutters and the customers they served. Just as important, from the point of view of custom cutters, was the relationship between their own two occupations, custom cutting and farming. Only a small elite among custom combiners did nothing else for a living. A few held some other job in the off-season, but the great majority were part-time farmers, part-time custom cutters. These were of two classes—winter wheat farmers and spring wheat farmers. Both classes fashioned their harvesting seasons in such a way that they also could get their farm work done at home.

This planning was easier for spring wheat farmers. After sowing their wheat, they had no major tasks to perform at home until harvest, and so they were free to head south as long as they returned in time to swath and combine their own crops. They only needed to arrange for someone, probably a member of the family, to take care of the livestock and a few chores.

For winter wheat farmers, the situation was more complicated. They were relatively free from major tasks on their farms in the spring until the harvest, but then there was plowing to do. Throughout the summer the plowed ground had to be worked after each rain. Some custom cutters therefore relied on other members of the family to do the field work at home while they moved on north. Fathers, sons, or wives assumed these tasks. In other cases some neighbor did the field work on a custom basis, or a man was hired to do it. Older farmers who were partly retired often were available for this sort of work. Another possibility was to release men from the harvest crew when it was necessary to do field work. A man or two might stay behind to finish the plowing after the rest of the crew moved on and then rejoin them when it was done. For the rest of the season, whenever men could be spared from the crew—especially during rainy spells—they would hurry home to work the ground and then rush back to the combines.

For both spring wheat farmers and winter wheat farmers, custom cutting took the place of any diversified farming that they might have considered in addition to small grains. Because summers were occupied with harvesting, custom cutters were not at home to irrigate, cultivate, or do any of the other tasks associated with diversified farming. All these things were possible only if there were enough members of the family who could remain at home to do them.

The economic reasons why men became custom cutters varied with the times. During the early years the motivation was simple opportunism, for it was obvious that profits were being made. The returning serviceman, the restless farmer, or any man on the make needed only a bit of capital and a few workers to get started. "No college education, I liked machinery, and custom combining seemed to be the coming thing," summed up one Kansan who started custom cutting in 1947.[15]

Farmers, since they owned the necessary machinery and had deferments from the draft, had the advantage in starting in the business. Interviews with seventy-one custom cutters in western Oklahoma in 1948 showed that forty-four of them also were farmers. Eleven held other occupations, including implement dealer, mechanic, truck driver, blacksmith, barber, schoolteacher, and even skating rink operator. Sixteen of the custom cutters said they were full-time, professional harvesters. The custom cutters who farmed had large farms for the times, averaging 650 acres, with 462 acres in wheat. Since some of the acreage must have been fallowed, it was obvious that these part-time farmers grew wheat and little else. Many of them stated that they planned to custom cut only long enough to pay for their combines. Others hoped to employ themselves profitably during the slack seasons of work that accompanied farming a single crop. It seemed sensible to put idle machinery and idle sons to work at such times.[16]

One particular group of industrious farmers contributed more than its share of recruits to the ranks of early custom cutters. Mennonites were conscientious objectors, and they had the men, machinery, and willingness to enter the business of custom combining during World War II. In 1942 investigators from the Economic Research Service compiled a map with dots showing points of origin for custom combines. A cluster of dots covered the area of Newton, Inman, and Moundridge, Kansas, where there were concentrations of Mennonites. The tradition of custom cutting established early continued among Mennonites of the area. Farmers considered Mennonites ideal custom cutters, honest and reliable.[17]

In time the element of opportunism in custom cutting diminished, as bad years drove out those who had entered the business in hopes of quick profits. This strengthened the relative role of part-time farmers in custom combining. People with other profitable occupations abandoned custom cutting; part-time farmers tried to make ends meet by working harder at both farming and harvesting. The Economic Research Service concluded that 91 percent of the custom cutters operating in 1971 were part-time farmers or ranchers.[18]

Entrants into the business during the 1950s and 1960s seemed less attracted to it than driven to it by poor conditions in agriculture. Asked why they began custom cutting, many answered that they turned to it as a last resort because they could not make a living on their farms. One custom cutting wife explained that she and her husband were unable to obtain land they needed for expansion "because of some farmers getting too hoggish," and so the alternative was custom cutting. "I couldn't get a hold of any more land and so I had to do something else," wrote another harvester. A third concurred: "My farming operation was not big enough to justify the cost of machinery and I could not rent more land so I went into this. Since we had four boys and one girl it worked out real good as a family operation."[19]

A farmer from Saskatchewan turned custom cutter when stifled by Canada's system of marketing quotas designed to maintain prices for grain. Under the Wheat Board's quotas he was permitted to market only six bushels from each cultivated acre. Custom cutting gave him an outlet for initiative when he had to cut back on farming.

Other custom cutters played variations on the same themes as to why they began in the business. "Could not afford to have those high price machines sitting around," noted one. Others hoped to make enough money custom cutting to purchase additional land or machinery. One quit farming and had three sons and two combines on his hands, making custom cutting a logical option. Another saw his corn-grinding business in Kansas declining and moved naturally into another line of custom work.[20]

The sad straits forcing farmers into custom cutting did not mean that entrepreneurism had vanished from the business. There still was the chance for an ambitious young man to use custom cutting as a vehicle to a better life. A good example was Loren Unruh of Great Bend, Kansas. He grew up on a farm west of there, and in 1963, after he had finished basic training for the Army Reserve, he began custom cutting with a single combine. He expanded his business ambitiously and eventually became a partner in an outfit of six machines. A practical businessman, he began custom combining with the goal of raising capital for other opportunities. First he bought additional farmland with his father, and then he opened a popular and successful steak house in Great Bend.[21]

Another young man made good was Ron Roessler, who grew up on a farm near Manhattan, Kansas. He had custom

Custom combiners like Clair Howe, kneeling in the stubble to replace a bearing on his augur shaft, boasted decades of experience in the business.

combined for a few years locally while a college student, but he gave it up in 1970 to go to graduate school in Iowa. There he saw so many combines standing idle in the summer, waiting for corn harvest, that he decided to put some of them to work. In the summer of 1971 he leased five combines and entered the harvest in Kansas. His first few years in the business were the makings of a textbook on how not to succeed as a custom cutter, but sympathetic bankers carried him through, and eventually he purchased his own combines. In so doing he proved that a young man with little capital could work his way into a business that required heavy investment.[22]

The custom cutters who lasted through hard times showed remarkable tenure in their business. More than 65 percent of the custom cutters surveyed by the Economic Research Service in 1971 had at least ten years' experience in the business. Only about one custom cutter in twenty had not custom cut for at least two years before. A survey of thirty-nine custom cutters in the harvest of 1977 showed that they had an average of more than fourteen years' experience.[23]

Not only did custom cutters remain in the business for long tenure, but they also brought up their sons to carry on in the trade. Nearly all custom outfits during the later years of the business contained two generations, and many benefited simultaneously from the experience of a grandfather, the vigor of sons, and the enthusiasm of grandsons. Daughters of custom cutters frequently lured their husbands into the business. Trusted employees sometimes worked their way into partnerships in custom outfits, but more often acquired their own machines and began on their own.

New generations of custom cutters knew the hectic days of the Harvest Brigade only by worn photographs and by stories that they grew tired of hearing. They entered the business by inheritance and thought of it as part of the natural order of affairs, not as merely a by-product of World War II. They were the best evidence that custom combining had become an established institution in the agricultural economy of the Great Plains.

Chapter 5
Pilgrim Capitalism
Aspects of a Peculiar Business

"My father started combining in 1947," wrote a frustrated custom cutter from Alva, Oklahoma, "when a new combine cost about $1,800 and he got around 4 or 5 dollars per acre for combining and hauling. Now [1977] my combines cost $38,000 and I get about $8 per acre for combining. It can't work no way, even if I cut more than he did." Added another combiner from Oklahoma City, "I have only been harvesting for six years, but in that short time my expenses have quadrupled."[1] As custom cutters looked forward to what they believed would be a disappointing season in 1977, they voiced a host of complaints. As had happened so often in the past, economic forces beyond their control had wrought turmoil in western agriculture and, indirectly, in custom cutting.

The business of custom combining enjoyed brief periods of prosperity, but most of the time custom cutters struggled against conditions like those in 1977 or worse. Rising expenses bumped up against static rates for harvesting. Only when farmers enjoyed prosperity could custom cutters push rates comfortably above expenses. Custom cutters whose skills of management were inadequate to carry them through hard times were blown out like chaff. Custom combining became the business of an elite among harvesters, pilgrim capitalists who developed the methods they needed to succeed and stamped their business as unique.

Custom combining was a business of individuals and of families. Few custom outfits were incorporated. State records of permits issued to custom harvesters showed hardly any machinery registered in the names of corporations, although some combines might have been recorded under the names of individuals but owned by corporations. Of forty custom cutters polled in 1977, only one had incorporated his operation.[2] When custom cutters chose to incorporate, rarely was it for the purpose of raising capital. Corporations were designed to permit members of the family a share in ownership, to integrate operations of farming and custom cutting, and to avoid disastrous inheritance taxes.

Partnerships were much more common among custom cutters than were corporations. Members of a family, most often fathers and sons, but frequently brothers, sometimes formed traditional types of partnerships with joint ownership of machinery. More commonly they formed working partnerships. This meant that they supplied machinery under individual ownership (for instance, a father and a son each owning a combine), but worked on jobs together and shared expenses and profits in proportion to the amount of machinery supplied by each. Working partnerships like this were common also among custom cutters who were not relatives. Occasionally, working partnerships were formed on an intermittent basis. Two custom cutters might agree to work together at certain stops on their routes, but to go their separate ways the rest of the time. This allowed them to form a large outfit to handle big jobs and to split up where the jobs were small. Custom cutters who ran their outfits by themselves, with no partners, assumed formidable duties. Situations that required them to deal with customers or other outsiders at the same time they supervised their crews arose continually.

The measure of a custom harvester was his combines. When asked how large his outfit was, a custom cutter would answer quickly with the number of machines he operated and perhaps the makes and models. When asked how many men were in his crew, if it was a large one, he would start counting them on his fingers.

Custom cutters wanted no more combines in their outfits than they could manage efficiently. It was not unusual for a custom cutter to purchase additional combines during good times, only to discover that he had more machines than he could handle, and to reduce the size of his outfit again. The level of greatest efficiency varied with individual talents, but for custom cutters as a class, certain sizes of outfits cut more acres to a machine than did others.

A study of custom outfits in Oklahoma in 1948 showed that custom cutters with the most combines planned to harvest more acres per combine than did those with fewer combines. Custom cutters with one or two combines in their outfits believed that they would cut about 1,800 acres to a machine in 1948. Custom cutters with more combines intended to cut 2,000 or more acres with each machine. Two circumstances might have tilted the balance in favor of the big operators in these estimates. Custom combiners with more than two machines usually were more experienced in the business than were those with only one or two and thus had more jobs arranged in advance. Also, since the figures recorded custom cutters' intentions and not acres actually cut, the bigger operators might have been bigger optimists than their fellows.[3]

Information gathered by the Economic Research Service in 1971 confirmed that, up to a point, the more combines in the outfit, the more acres each machine cut. This was to be expected, for the smaller outfits also worked shorter seasons. Efficiency began to decrease, however, with the addition of the fifth combine to an outfit. The acres cut by each machine were fewest with the largest outfits. Such large enterprises apparently presented too many problems of management to keep all the machines running constantly (see table 6).[4]

Thirty-two custom cutters who reported the acreage they intended to cut in 1977 confirmed the general trends shown in 1971, with some variations. Custom cutters with two combines in their outfits planned to cut nearly 2,600 acres to a combine for the season, with the acres distributed among stops on the route to an average of 452 acres to a combine at each stop. Custom cutters with three combines reported great expectations. They intended to cut nearly 4,000 acres to each combine, which figured out to nearly 550 acres to a combine for each stop. This category happened to include a few

Table 6.

Acres Combined per Machine by Different
Sizes of Custom Outfits, 1971

Number of Combines in Outfit	Average Number of Acres Combined per Machine
1	1,682
2	1,845
3	1,907
4	2,062
5	2,023
6	1,829
7	2,014
8	1,572
9	no cases
10 or more	1,474
all outfits	1,971

Source: Lagrone and Gavett, *Interstate Custom Combining in the Great Plains in 1971.*

operators with long routes and extended seasons. Custom cutters with four or more combines expected to harvest only about 2,200 acres to each combine, about 300 acres at each stop.[5]

Perhaps combines in larger outfits cut more acres, at least up to a point, but the average number of combines operated by custom cutters remained low. Most custom harvesters fielded only one or two combines. Unknown, however, was how many of these custom combiners recorded in various records as individual operators joined with others to form working partnerships, thus making larger outfits but keeping separate rate ownership.

Custom cutters with single combines were most numerous in the initial years of the business. The typical outfit found working in Nebraska in 1942 was a single twelve-foot drag machine, a tractor, a truck, and three men. Hardly any outfits

107

had more than one combine. By 1948 combiners in Oklahoma showed the effects of a few years' expansion, since among those surveyed were a substantial number of outfits with two or three machines. Twenty custom cutters had one machine, twenty-three had two machines, and fifteen had three machines. The greatest number of combines in one outfit was nine, but the average number was 2.5. The information indicated that custom cutters with several combines generally had started in previous years with only one and had added machines one at a time.[6]

The mode of two machines to an outfit was more than just a stage in the expansion of the industry; it developed into the standard size of custom outfits through the years, at least as measured by the number of combines to an owner and disregarding hidden working partnerships. According to records of weed inspections in Nebraska, the average number of combines for custom cutters entering the state in 1969 was 2.2. Two combines to an owner was the modal size, but operators

Table 7.

Size of Custom Outfits in Nebraska, 1969

Number of Combines per Outfit	Number of Outfits	% of Outfits	% of Combines
1	505	26.3	11.9
2	834	43.5	39.2
3	341	17.8	24.1
4	166	8.7	15.6
5	47	2.5	5.5
6	21	1.1	3.0
7	3	.2	.5
8	1	.1	.8
	1,918		

Source: Noxious Weeds Division, Bureau of Plant Industry, Nebraska State Department of Agriculture.

Table 8.

Size of Custom Outfits, 1971

Number of Combines per Outfit	Number of Outfits	% of Outfits	% of Combines
1	961	28.0	12.77
2	1,466	42.7	38.8
3	610	17.8	24.2
4	264	7.7	14.0
5	64	1.9	4.2
6	38	1.1	3.0
7	10	.3	.9
8	12	.3	1.3
9	0	.0	.0
10 or more	6	.2	.9
	3,431		

Source: Lagrone and Gavett, *Interstate Custom Combining in the Great Plains in 1971.*

with single machines also were numerous. Custom cutters with three or four machines apiece controlled more combines as a group than did those with only one apiece, however (see table 7).[7]

The Economic Research Service in 1971 found the same average of 2.2 combines to an owner among all custom cutters. The distribution of combines per outfit was quite similar to that in Nebraska in 1969 (see table 8).[8]

Information taken from harvesters' permits in the files of the Montana Department of Highways revealed that in 1976, 2.1 combines to an outfit was the average for custom cutters working in the state. There was a greater proportion of custom cutters with only one machine and a smaller proportion of them with two (see table 9).[9]

The indication from all this was that, although there were a few big operators on the road, most custom cutters remained

Table 9.

Size of Custom Outfits in Montana, 1976

Number of Combines per outfit	Number of Outfits	% of Outfits	% of Combines
1	207	34.3	15.8
2	224	37.1	34.3
3	104	17.2	23.9
4	35	5.8	10.7
5	18	3.0	6.9
6	9	1.5	4.1
7	1	.2	.5
8	1	.2	.6
9	2	.3	1.4
10	1	.2	.8
11	1	.2	.8
	603		

Source: Montana Department of Highways.

small-time capitalists. Working partnerships no doubt raised the effective size of many outfits, and larger outfits had importance beyond their numbers, for they controlled proportionally more of the number of combines than they did the number of outfits.

The number of combines to an outfit varied little with the state of origin. In Nebraska in 1969 each of the five states of origin that supplied the bulk of the custom combines averaged between 2.0 and 2.4 machines to an outfit. Outfits from Texas averaged the largest. For all custom outfits surveyed in 1971, the eight states providing the great majority of the machines averaged between 2.1 and 2.4 combines to an outfit. In this case outfits from Texas were of about average size, and outfits from North Dakota were the largest. Likewise, returns for Montana in 1976 showed that the principal states of origin sent outfits averaging from 2.0 to 2.2 combines apiece. If in these several instances there were differences among the states of origin in the average size of outfits, the differences were less important than the similarities. In all cases the typical size of outfit was two combines, and the average size was slightly more.[10]

Although state of origin made little difference in the size of outfit, the area in which the outfit worked was important. Custom cutters working on the high western plains, where farms were larger, themselves had larger outfits than harvesters farther east. Custom cutters entering Nebraska in 1969 through western ports of entry had more combines on the average than did those entering through eastern ports (see Figure 12). In both the west and the east the typical outfit was two machines, but in the west there were more outfits with three or more machines, while in the east there were more with only one combine. The four ports farthest east admitted almost as many outfits with one combine as with two. Smaller outfits to the east were suitable for the smaller jobs found there; large outfits found sufficient work only where acreages were large.[11]

By the same logic it would have been expected that outfits in Montana would be larger than the average also, but this was not the case, at least not in 1976. Custom cutters in Montana in 1976 averaged only 2.1 combines apiece, mainly because there were so many custom cutters with only one combine. Probably custom outfits working in the northern plains averaged somewhat smaller than those farther south. In South Dakota in the same year, there were no records of the number of combines in each outfit, but custom cutters there averaged only 1.7 trucks apiece. Almost as many custom cutters had only one truck as had two, and, no doubt, some of the operators with two trucks had only one combine.[12]

However many combines custom cutters included in their outfits, they also had to make provisions to haul the grain they cut. In the earliest years of the industry, many custom cutters did not do their own hauling. They either relied on the farmers they cut for to haul the grain or allied themselves with owners of trucks in working partnerships, the custom cutters

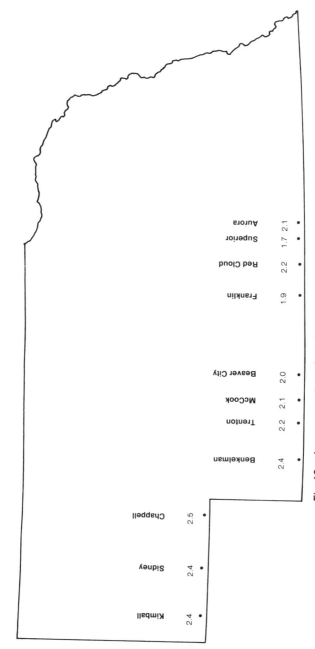

Fig. 12. Average number of combines per outfit at ports of entry in Nebraska, 1969. Data from Noxious Weeds Division, Bureau of Plant Industry, Nebraska State Department of Agriculture.

receiving the revenues for combining, the truckers the charges for hauling. This kind of arrangement died out completely by the mid-1950s, and thereafter custom cutters included in their outfits about one grain truck for every combine.

The hauling capacity of the trucks increased with the cutting capacity of the combines through the years. Among custom cutters as a group there always were a few more trucks than combines, for a few operators took one more truck than they had combines in order to keep up with the hauling more easily. In 1971, 3,431 custom cutters surveyed had 7,946 grain trucks, an average of 2.3 apiece, as compared to the average of 2.2 combines. Custom cutters in Montana in 1976 also had 2.3 grain trucks to the outfit, compared to 2.1 combines. Thus, custom cutters in South Dakota in the same year, with only 1.7 trucks to the outfit, probably had even fewer combines to the outfit.[13]

Some custom cutters augmented their capacity for carrying grain with special equipment. A few took grain carts to be drawn behind tractors. These were used not to haul grain to the elevator, but to haul it in the field from the combines to the trucks. This was useful when soft ground or mud prevented the trucks from reaching the combines, but grain carts and tractors were too much trouble to transport for most operators. Others took pup trailers, which they either hitched singly behind heavy grain trucks or coupled two at a time behind semitractor cabs. A few used semitrailers or gravel trucks for hauling. All these methods were uncommon exceptions.

Custom cutters from the winter wheat regions who cut their way into the spring wheat regions took along pickup headers to handle windrowed grain. Thirty-eight custom cutters surveyed in 1977 owned 120 combines, but only 82 pickup headers.[14] Custom cutters who could arrange suitable routes without any pickup work did so. Not only were they averse to transporting pickup headers and putting them on the combines, but also harvesters accustomed to straight-cutting just disliked picking up grain from the windrow. They complained that farmers did not stay far enough ahead in the

Combines of the Ruben White outfit dump on the go in western Oklahoma, 1977.

work of windrowing to keep them constantly employed, and they doubted that they could cover as many acres of wind-rows as of standing grain. They complained loudest when they inadvertently picked up rocks or skunks in the windrow and ran them through the combine. On the other hand, custom cutters coming from the spring wheat region to harvest on the southern plains had to buy sickle headers for straight-cutting.

A custom outfit needed some sort of service vehicle containing equipment for maintenance. Usually this equipment was carried in a trailer, but often a one-ton truck or three-quarter-ton pickup served the purpose. In the 1940s a few custom cutters even used army surplus maintenance trucks. A well-equipped custom outfit carried a welder, a cutting torch, and an air compressor in the service vehicle, as well as hand tools and grease guns. In boxes and cabinets were stored several thousand dollars' worth of parts for the combines. In 1971, 3,431 outfits reported that they had 2,092 service trailers and 761 service trucks.[15]

Most custom cutters also considered pickup trucks necessities. They needed pickups for fast trips to and from and around the field. They also carried supplies of diesel fuel—gasoline in earlier years—in rectangular tanks mounted in the beds of the pickups next to the cabs. They pumped fuel from these tanks to the combines with electric pumps powered by the pickup batteries, or in earlier years with hand pumps. In 1971, 3,431 custom cutters reported that they used 3,052 pickup trucks. Custom cutters whose families accompanied them on the harvest also generally took automobiles. Thirty-nine custom cutters surveyed in 1977 traveled with 58 pickup trucks and 21 automobiles.[16]

Standard equipment for nearly all custom outfits by the late 1960s were two-way radios, sometimes business band, but usually citizen's band. Custom cutters in the 1970s equipped nearly every vehicle and combine with a CB. Thirty-seven custom cutters in 1977 reported that they used 307 two-way radios, 275 citizen's band, and 32 business band.[17]

Individual custom cutters often took along additional equipment to suit their needs or fancies. Before the adoption of self-propelled combines, tractors accompanied each outfit. When tractors no longer were needed to draw combines, a few custom cutters continued to take them along to pull stuck vehicles from the mud. Occasionally, a motorcycle would be seen strapped to a trailer. A handful of custom cutters used airplanes to scout jobs and to fetch parts. A plane parked in the stubble field among the combines and trucks made an incongruous sight.

Transporting all this equipment, especially the combines, sometimes taxed the resourcefulness of custom cutters. To transport the pull-type combines used in the 1940s down the highways, custom cutters first loaded the tractors into the beds of the grain trucks. Then they disconnected the headers

Pete Peters, custom cutter from Hastings, Nebraska, in 1940 used a variety of trailers and loading arrangements to transport his combines.
Photo courtesy of Pete Peters.

from the combines and hitched the combines behind the grain trucks. Finally they loaded the headers onto trailers that they hitched behind the combines. Those custom cutters without trucks had to make their slow way north pulling their combines behind their tractors.

Early self-propelled combines fourteen feet or less in width could be loaded fully assembled onto the beds of grain trucks. This was a handy way to travel, but a risky one. The loaded truck was top-heavy and therefore dangerous in high winds, on inclines, or on curves. Protruding headers atop the trucks were a fearsome sight to oncoming motorists. Signposts at the edge of the road sometimes fell victim to headers extending to the side, especially Massey-Harris headers, which were offset to the right. The bane of custom cutters traveling in this fashion was overpasses, which frequently swept protruding grain shafts from atop combines.

Headers wider than fourteen feet had to be detached and

116

placed on trailers behind the trucks. In the 1960s, as weights and wheel bases of combines increased, it became too unwieldy and dangerous to load them onto trucks. Custom cutters then began to experiment with building trailers to hold the combines and loading the headers into the truck beds. Among the innovators were the members of the Jantz family of Moundridge, Kansas, who in 1967 abandoned custom cutting to form a company to manufacture combine trailers. Their chief competitor was Donahue Corporation of Donahue, Kansas, established about the same time.[18] Combine trailers, homemade or purchased, became standard equipment. Finally headers became too long to haul in truck beds, and so custom cutters began placing them on header trailers pulled behind pickups or service trucks.

Pete Peters's outfit in 1952 loaded its fourteen-foot No. 27 Massey-Harris combines on trucks for transportation.
Photo courtesy of Pete Peters.

Most custom cutters liked new machinery. There was a certain amount of pure vanity in the desires of harvesters to parade caravans of the latest models of combines and trucks down the main streets of the little towns they passed through. Beyond this there was the effect of appearing substantial and well equipped to potential customers. Farmers often chose harvesters by appearance, and they also had their vanity, for they wanted to hire sharp-looking outfits.

Some custom cutters adhered to regular schedules of how often to trade their combines and trucks for new ones, but most made these decisions by the nature of the times and the opportunity of the moment. Any time a favorable trade could be made was the time to make it. When business was good, as it was from 1973 to 1976, custom cutters traded more often. The Economic Research Service in 1971 found that custom cutters kept their combines for an average of 3.8 years before trading. The number of years of use varied inversely with the length of the harvesting season for the outfits. In Montana in 1976, 77 percent of the combines used by custom cutters were 1974 models or newer. More than one-third were 1976 models, and only about one in twenty was older than a 1970 model. Combines thus were of recent vintage, but it was not the policy of most custom cutters to trade every year.[19]

Custom cutters kept trucks longer before trading than they did combines because trucks were less subject to wear than combines. The average age of trucks in Montana in 1976 was 4.5 years, as compared to 2.6 years for combines. Only one truck in nine was a 1976 model. One 1949 model was in use. In South Dakota in 1976 the trucks were a bit older on the average, 5.0 years, but there was about the same proportion of 1976 models as in Montana. The same 1949 truck showed up in South Dakota.[20]

Custom harvesters frequently argued the merits of various makes of combines, but they seldom changed each other's minds. Custom cutters generally owned combines all of the same make, and rarely did they switch brands. The custom cutter who learned to operate, service, and repair one make of combine was reluctant to switch to another, and, besides, custom cutters tended to trade with the same dealer repeatedly in order to be assured of fair dealing and good service. When Elmer Dirks of Buhler, Kansas, a custom cutter since 1947, switched from Massey-Ferguson combines to John Deere, it was an event notable enough to merit a story in John Deere's *Furrow* magazine with the heading, "The Switch Is On!" His son Keith, however, remained a Massey man.[21] In unguarded moments, custom cutters admitted that the merits of the various makes of combines were close. Rarely was a significant improvement by one implement company not soon adopted by the others.

After World War II and the Harvest Brigade, Massey-Harris (Massey-Ferguson), with its self-propelled models, had the advantage over other implement companies in sales to custom cutters. Gleaner-Baldwin and John Deere soon followed with successful self-propelled models. Gleaner-Baldwin, later to become a subsidiary of Allis-Chalmers Corporation, seemed to overtake the initial advantage of Massey-Harris among custom cutters in the 1950s. Custom cutters liked the compact frame of the Gleaner for hauling and disliked certain innovations made in Massey-Ferguson's design. In 1969, 42 percent of the custom combines operating in Nebraska were Gleaners, 29 percent were Masseys, and 21 percent were John Deeres. The few remaining were distributed among makes that never captured a significant share of the custom cutters' market, such as Case, International Harvester, and Oliver. Of the custom combines in Montana in 1976, 39 percent were Gleaners, 27 percent were Masseys, and 30 percent were John Deeres.[22]

Custom cutters stood to benefit when implement companies actively sought their business. Allis-Chalmers and Massey-Ferguson sent mobile units into the wheat belt during harvest to provide parts, repairs, and counsel to custom cutters when they could not get them from local dealers. These units followed the harvest north and parked in towns where they were needed. Certain implement dealers, such as Joe Vater of Enid, Oklahoma, specialized in sales to custom cutters.[23]

In 1949 the Peters custom outfit, then making the transition from pull-type combines to self-propelled machines, included this tractor-drawn unit.
Photo courtesy of Pete Peters.

Improvements in combines since the founding of the custom cutting industry were dramatic. Only about 2 percent of the custom combines in Nebraska in 1942 were self-propelled. Most of the rest of the combines, drag machines, had cutter bars of only eleven or twelve feet. A few were tiny power takeoff models designed for use in the Midwest.[24]

The first great change in combines for custom cutters was the transition from drag combines to self-propelled machines. This transition received a boost from the publicity accorded the Massey-Harris Self-propelled Harvest Brigade. Decades later old custom cutters still fondly remembered the Massey-Harris No. 21A and No. 27, but John Deere launched its self-propelled No. 55 in 1947, and other companies followed suit.

During the early 1950s custom cutters rapidly replaced drag machines with self-propelled combines, which not only required fewer men to operate but also were more convenient for traveling.

In succeeding years technological development of combines did nothing to change their basic principles, but combines became larger and more efficient. The first Massey-Harris self-propelled models had cutter bars of twelve or fourteen feet, but John Deere started out with a sixteen-foot model. Thereafter the increase in size proceeded slowly. By 1971, 57 percent of all custom combines had headers of twenty

Dale Peters (Pete's half-brother) drove this Massey-Harris No. 21A self-propelled combine in 1949.
Photo courtesy of Pete Peters.

feet, and 23 percent more had headers of eighteen feet. By 1977, twenty-four-foot headers were the most common size, with twenty-foot nearly as popular. The implement companies fielded experimental models that cut thirty-foot swaths.[25]

Much additional improvement in combines resulted from the suggestions and complaints of custom cutters. Early self-propelled combines had tires so small that they quickly became mired in soft ground or mud, especially when the grain tanks were full. Custom cutters obtained used bomber tires from military surplus and enlarged their combine wheel frames to fit them, alleviating their problems with mud. A machine shop in Wichita, the air capital, made this modification its specialty. Implement companies soon offered larger tires as standard equipment.[26] Custom cutters demanded combines built low enough to the ground to pass safely through highway underpasses. They wanted headers that could be detached and put back on quickly. They called for machines with better balance, more reliability, greater capacity, powerful engine, and variable transmission. All these improvements, when embraced by implement companies, benefited farmers as well as custom cutters.

The greatest proof of the leading role played by custom harvesters in improving combines was that each year the major implement companies placed their experimental model combines in the hands of professional custom cutters, where they would get the most grueling use. Engineers from the companies followed the experimental machines through the harvest to make necessary adjustments and to note how the combines might be modified to suit harvesters' needs.

Improvements and enlargements of grain trucks kept pace with development of combines. In the early 1940s most trucks were 1-ton or 1½-ton Fords or Chevrolets. Most custom cutters recalled getting the first hydraulic lifts on their trucks around 1947 or 1948. The bed lengths and hauling capacities of the bobtail trucks used by custom cutters increased until, in the late 1960s, they began to switch from single-axle to tandem-axle ("twin-screw") trucks. By the mid-1970s most custom outfits relied on tandem-axle trucks or a mixture of tandem-axle and single-axle trucks. Tandem-axle trucks had greater capacity, but some part-time farmers reasoned that ordinary bobtail trucks were more practical for general use around the farm.

Almost 70 percent of the trucks used by thirty-nine custom cutters surveyed in 1977 were tandem-axle or tri-axle models. Most had twenty-foot beds, and the average capacity was nearly 600 bushels. Single-axle trucks at the same time mostly had beds of sixteen feet, and their average capacity was about 350 bushels. Chevrolet trucks were the overwhelming favorite among custom cutters in 1976, at least those working in Montana and South Dakota. About half the trucks used were Chevrolets, about a fifth were Fords, about an eighth were GMCs, and about a tenth were International Harvesters.[27]

Because machines and equipment were such an important part of custom cutters' operations, the cutters lavished care upon them. Regular maintenance was part of the routine, and woe to the hand who failed to grease every zerk on the machine before starting up. Before loading up to move to another stop, custom cutters often ran their outfits through coin-operated car washes. Ted Hardwick of Saxmon, Kansas, showed how meticulous a custom cutter could be about his equipment. During rainy spells his crewmen not only washed the combines but also waxed them, a job that must have made them hope for good cutting weather again. Each morning the men hosed out the radiators on the combines and trucks with water and blew out the cabs with an air compressor. Hardwick insisted that no objects clutter the floorboards of the trucks except water jugs. During the winter, when the combines were in storage, he put mothballs in the cabs.[28] Measures like these might have been expected to provoke discontent among workers, but such was not the case. Workers on most outfits tended to become attached to the particular machines they regularly operated. They sometimes gave them names and became fanatical about their care. Besides, those laborers who were paid by the hour were happy to log some hours cleaning up the machinery on rainy days.

Loving care of machinery was symbolically appropriate, for

with each passing year custom cutting became more capital-intensive. With bigger and better machines—and more expensive ones—fewer men accomplished the same amount of work. In the days of drag combines, three workers were needed for each machine—one to drive the tractor, one to handle the combine, and the third to drive the truck. Self-propelled combines eliminated the need for a tractor driver. Then the increasing size of self-propelled combines gradually reduced the total number of combines needed, incidentally also reducing the total number of workers required.

In Nebraska in 1942, when nearly all custom combines were drag machines, outfits averaged about 2.7 men to each combine. Although some crews must have had extra men besides the three who would be expected with each combine, the average was fewer than three men to a combine because some outfits still traveled without trucks. A few of the combines also were power takeoff models that required no man riding on the combine. Much later, in Nebraska in 1969, custom outfits averaged only 1.8 men to a combine. Self-propelled combines obviously had decreased the need for laborers, but in addition, some outfits apparently were operating with fewer truck drivers than they had trucks, letting the drivers shuttle the trucks from field to elevator.[29]

Such statistics presented but part of the story, for they considered only laborers in the field with the machines and not attendant workers, such as cooks. After the first few years of the business, the cooking and housekeeping for custom outfits usually was done by wives and other members of the families of custom cutters. The Economic Research Service included these domestic workers from the family in its calculations to discover that custom crews in 1971 averaged about 2.2 workers to a combine. The same study showed that the larger the outfit, the easier it was to manage with fewer crewmen to the combine by cutting down on truck drivers.[30]

The survey in 1971 also illustrated the blend of hired laborers and family members that went into the composition of custom crews. Sixteen percent of the outfits, most of them with one or two combines, used only the labor of family mem-

In 1977, Neva Elmore cooked for a custom crew of thirty men.

bers in 1971. Seventeen percent of the outfits, generally among the largest, used only hired labor. The remainder used both. Among thirty-nine outfits surveyed in 1977, hired labor predominated, with 176 hired workers and 105 family members manning the crews. There were more hired workers than family members working on all sizes of outfits.[31]

125

Although hired men outnumbered family members in the ranks of harvesters, the family members were a peculiar and important part of the crews. They constituted cheap labor that did not have to be recruited, without which many custom cutters could not operate. It certainly would have been too expensive for most custom cutters to hire full-time cooks, but wives served admirably, and the price was right. Family members also were more devoted to the work at hand, because custom cutting was the business of the entire family. In this way custom cutting was similar to its host industry, farming.

Obtaining enough good hired workers always was a concern of custom cutters. During World War II custom cutters had to hire whomever they could find, and, at least according to their accounts, they ended up with far too many drunks and deadbeats. Crewmen of this time also were conspicuous for their age. Men who otherwise might have been considered retired, attracted by rising wages, went on the harvest during that time of emergency. Immediately after the war there were more men of all ages available for employment, but custom cutters found that they had to choose between older men and younger ones and hire all of one or the other. With some exceptions, older men and teenagers got along poorly in the same crew. Custom cutters therefore chose youthful enthusiasm over wizened experience. From the 1950s on, custom cutters tended more and more to hire young men in their teens or early twenties, most often students working through the summer. If they were inexperienced, they also were quick to learn. The great disadvantage in hiring students was that they returned to school in September. Custom cutters who worked through the fall therefore generally curtailed their operations and ran fewer machines in the fall harvest. If possible, they recruited additional workers from local populations.

Custom cutters usually hired workers from their own localities, from families they knew personally. They especially hoped to seduce farm boys who were familiar with harvesting machinery into making the harvest with them. Most custom

This custom crew in Colorado in 1948 differed substantially in average age from modern crews, which are composed mainly of students.
Photo courtesy of Elmer Graffis.

cutters had no formal process for interviewing workers or weighing their qualifications. Only the most meticulous took written applications for work. One who did sent each applicant a statement about custom combining in order to help the prospective employee decide whether the job was for him. "This is quite a different type of work than most jobs," he asserted in a masterpiece of understatement. The questions he then asked of applicants were designed to weed out any potential sources of difficulty. Inquiries dealt with smoking, drinking, drugs, allergies, and criminal records. Then there was the pivotal question, "Do you like to work around machinery, cars and motors?"[32]

Crewmen of the Ruben White outfit join forces to replace a broken sickle.

Custom cutters with sons in high school or college often used them to screen or recommend employees. Other custom cutters advertised for help in agricultural periodicals, regional newspapers, or college campus newspapers. The advertiser might seek a certain type of employee by advertising in a particular publication. Some Mennonite custom cutters from Kansas advertised for help in denominational magazines, thereby recruiting farm boys from Pennsylvania eager for a summer on the plains.

When custom cutters during the later years were asked what the greatest problem of their business was, they almost invariably answered, "getting good help." This was partly the result of general changes in society. There were fewer farmers, and thus fewer farm youths experienced with machinery to recruit. Youths from more affluent families were reluctant to take such strenuous work for the summer.

Yet the problem of "getting good help" arose at least partly from the rising expectations of custom cutters themselves. Certainly the laborers available in the early years of the industry were less than choice, but then there were fewer complaints about their fitness. It was one thing to put an inexperienced hand on a $4,000 combine and take a chance that he might do something foolish, however, and quite another to put the same novice on a $40,000 machine. The spiraling cost of machinery made it increasingly important that workers be knowledgeable and responsible. Custom cutters became less tolerant of learning by trial and error. Inexperienced hands received stern lectures on proper operation of equipment and were broken into the job under careful supervision.

Most of the hired youths who made up custom combine crews were students who needed money to stake another year in school. College students were the favored workers, but high school students, some of them as young as fifteen or sixteen, were equally numerous. A few custom cutters in the 1970s hired young women as truck drivers, but so few that they were an oddity. Most of the workers who were not going to school nevertheless were similar to them in that they were young and they worked the harvest only temporarily. For most all of the workers, custom cutting for a summer was a brief encounter with an interesting business, but little more than that. It furnished them with a little bit of money and a great store of anecdotes, but then they went on with their lives as usual.

If the deck of hired hands was largely of the same suit, there were enough wild cards to make the game interesting. Among them might be found the likes of a fellow from Michigan working the harvest to make money to buy farmland at his home, where he and his wife planned one day to own "the biggest damn farm in northern Michigan." Another was the son of the owner of a jeans factory in Lexington, Kentucky, and a senior at the University of Kentucky. His father had made the harvest decades earlier with an outfit from Oklahoma and wanted his son to have the same experience, "to make a man of him." The son was working for the same family of custom cutters that his father had. There was even a youth released from reform school into the custody of a custom cutter, to keep him busy for the summer.

Wages for hired hands never were princely, but because of the terms of employment and the type of work, laborers had the chance to save a good stake from a summer's work. The employers provided room and board, and so what wages the men made were pure profit, except for small personal expenses. If the idleness of too many rainy days did not tempt the men to frivolous spending, they could save most of the money they made.

No agency made any comprehensive record of wages paid to workers in custom outfits from year to year. In 1948 the most common wage was about a dollar an hour. Since most custom cutters also were farmers, wages on the harvest probably were comparable to those for other types of agricultural labor. Reports from custom harvesters in 1977 indicated that wages varied both in terms of payment and in amounts paid. The most common method of payment was a monthly wage. The monthly stipend varied greatly both among and within outfits, from about $450 to $1,500. About $700 seemed to be the usual monthly wage, but experience and age made great differences in the wages of workers. An inexperienced high school student could not expect top wages; he not only contributed less to the outfit, but also took up the time of other members who had to teach him the ropes. On the other hand, some workers, usually older men, not students, were of such value that they commanded premiums. They had years of experience and were skilled mechanics. Several custom cutters reported paying a weekly wage of $130 or so instead of a monthly wage. One offered $1,250 for the entire harvesting season, in his case about two months.[33]

Monthly, weekly, or seasonal wages had good and bad points. If the weather was good throughout the season, then these arrangements worked to the benefit of employers. No matter how many consecutive days the men worked, or how long the hours were, wages remained the same. If there were long spells of wet weather, then the workers benefited. They drew the same pay whether they worked in the field or played cards in the trailer.

Other custom cutters paid their men by the hour. In these cases the conservative employer was assured that he would not have to pay for men who were idle. Some ambitious crewmen also preferred this arrangement, for they hoped that the weather would remain good and they would log long hours. Hourly wages in 1977 generally were about $3.00 or $3.50 for most young hands, with better rates for experienced men. In some cases custom cutters gave their employees double assurance of fair returns: they stipulated payment by the hour, but with the provision that should the crew be idle too much, then the men still would receive a set amount each week or month. One custom cutter even worked out a plan replacing wages with shares in the outfit's revenues, granting each worker 3 to 5 percent of the gross income of the outfit. Most custom cutters paid a bonus to hands who lasted the whole season.[34]

Wages paid to laborers were one of many expenses that custom cutters balanced against revenues. Expenses for custom cutters increased gradually until the 1970s, when they spurted upward. From 1948 on, custom cutters fought the tightening grip of rising expenses and sliding revenues. Except perhaps in the first few years of the business, the most common size of outfit on the road was two combines. For such a typical enterprise profits declined through most of the history of custom cutting, but for an established operation with secure jobs to fill the season, decent returns remained possible.

Twenty-three operators of custom outfits with two combines each supplied information on their expenses to a researcher in western Oklahoma in 1948. The average number of acres they intended to cut in a season was 3,701 for each outfit. This estimate was for wheat only. If they cut the number of acres they intended to and received the going rate of the times for their work, $3.50, then the average income for base charges should have been almost $13,000 to an outfit. Assuming that the wheat cut yielded twenty bushels to the acre, then hauling charges figured at five cents a bushel boosted the average income of the outfits by about $3,700. Allowing a bit more income for charges for high yields, custom cutters with two combines should have expected an average gross income in the neighborhood of $17,000.

Against this income were pitted a variety of expenses. The study of 1948 recorded only expenses related to combining grain and not to hauling it. Custom cutters estimated their seasonal expenses for moving from stop to stop, as well as their expenses in the field for such items as repairs, gasoline, oil, and grease. They supplied estimates of the amount they paid for labor, and labor by members of the family was figured at a dollar an hour. Costs for depreciation of combines and interest on capital invested were included, the average investment in an outfit totaling $14,275. All told, the expenses considered averaged $7,557 a season for an outfit with two combines, or $2.04 for each acre cut. Costs for trucking would have added to this total considerably, although they would have been much lower than those for combining. Trucks required less fuel, labor, maintenance, and investment than combines. Costs of trucking should not have exceeded $3,000 for an outfit of two units. This would have meant total expenses for an outfit of two combines of some $10,500, to be subtracted from gross income of about $17,000.[35]

A net return of nearly $6,500 for a summer's work in 1948 was impressive, especially considering that the costs figured for the labor of family members would not have been paid out. Some custom cutters also would have supplemented what they made from the wheat harvest with additional work in the fall harvest. If custom combiners cut the acreage that they estimated they would in 1948, they earned fine profits. The problem for the business as a whole in 1948, and for years thereafter, was that too little work was available for most outfits to cut 3,700 acres in a season. The high returns possible if work could be found, however, explained why it was difficult for the business to adjust to a reduced demand for harvesting after 1948. Marginal custom cutters knew that profits were possible if only they could find work.

Information on earnings and costs of custom cutters gathered by the Economic Research Service in 1972 permitted some comparison with earlier conditions, although revenues and expenses were calculated in different ways than in the study of 1948. Researchers obtained business records for 1972 from a number of custom outfits, including ten with two combines each, still the most common size of outfit. The study found that the ten outfits cut an average of 4,146 acres of all crops for the year. Most of this, 3,250 acres, was wheat, and other small grains accounted for 339 acres. The only other crop with a large share of the average was milo, with 482 acres. Acreages of corn and other crops were much lower. The study recorded the rates obtained for all cutting, which for small grains usually were three-fifty, five, and five or four, five, and five. The average gross income for outfits with two combines was $24,443—$17,089 in base charges for combining, $5,707 for hauling, $1,059 for high yields, and $588 for miscellaneous income. This was a gross income of $5.86 for each acre cut.

Only cash expenses were considered in the study. No amounts were figured for depreciation of machinery, interest on investment, or value of family labor. Cash expenses for outfits with two combines averaged $11,518—$3,096 for wages, $2,426 for fuel, oil and grease, $2,314 for parts and service, and $3,682 for other expenses, including food, lodging, taxes, insurance, interest, and other small expenses. Expenses figured out to $3.36 an acre. The average net return over cash expenses was $12,925 for the season, or $2.50 an acre.[36]

Profits for custom cutting in 1972 were less satisfactory than those in 1948. Gross income had increased by nearly 50 percent, but this was too little to compensate for the declining value of the dollar, let alone to offset increased expenses. The returns above cash expenses generally represented the reward for the work of an entire family through the season,

Men and machines of the Bernel Elmore outfit prepare for a day's work in a north Texas wheat field infested with wild oats, 1977.

work demanding long hours and constant travel. The outfits also contributed an average of $37,804 in capital invested in equipment that depreciated rapidly.

Considering all this, there was still enough possibility of profit to explain why custom cutting had endured through the years. For most custom cutters, custom harvesting was just part of an operation that also included farming, and so it should not have been expected to provide net income commensurate to that expected of a full year's enterprise. Equipment used in custom harvesting also was used at home on the farm, and part of the expense of maintaining the outfit therefore should have been charged against the farm rather than the custom outfit. The portion of returns above cash expenses realized as profit by any custom cutter depended on his own financial skills, but the spread between gross income and cash expenses was enough to permit the survival of the business.

The economic development of custom combining from 1973 to 1976, stimulated by the rapid rise in the price of wheat, was so sudden and chaotic as almost to defy measurement. There were no comprehensive studies of rises in income and expenses during this time, but both were obvious. Rates charged for combining more than doubled at the same time that the amount of wheat available for harvesting increased, and so gross income skyrocketed. So did expenses, however. A spot survey of certain major items of expense in 1977 made this plain. Thirteen operators of outfits with two combines each said that they expected to pay total wages of $6,350 to an outfit, more than double the amount for wages reported by outfits of the same size in 1972. Rises in costs for fuel were even more striking, as custom cutters in 1977 expected to consume an average value of $6,207 in fuel, nearly three times what they spent in 1972. Prices for models of combines designed for the wheat belt advanced from about $15,000 to $35,000 or $40,000.

Just how far gross income outstripped rising expenses was unknown, but custom cutters certainly enjoyed unprecedented prosperity. They invested much of their newfound wealth in new and larger machinery, which in turn helped them to cover more acres. The average number of acres covered by outfits with two combines in 1977, according to custom cutters' expectations, was 6,087—5,222 acres of wheat, 444 acres of milo, and 421 acres of other crops.[37]

The meaning of the harvest of 1977 was unclear, for custom cutters themselves were not sure how it would affect their profits. Most ventured opinions that both rates and demand for cutting would decrease. The decreases that occurred were small, however, and for most custom cutters with established routes, the harvest of 1977 was business as usual. Probably, it was concern for the future that inspired most of the fears of custom cutters at this time. They had seen by previous experience that as long as the price of wheat remained low, they had little chance of passing along their increased expenses to farmers. They had been unable to do so from 1948 to 1972. In 1977 the market for wheat had been shattered, and there was no hope in sight of any relief.

If historical precedent was any indication, then what custom cutters faced in years to come was not a sudden drop in rates for cutting, but some reduction in the amount of work available. This was not likely to cause as much hardship as it had in decades earlier, for in the 1970s expansion had come with the enlargement of existing outfits more than with the addition of new ones, and so custom cutters should have been able to survive contractions of demand by sticking with their regular customers. What custom cutters could expect was a gradual belt-tightening. Expenses could not continue to rise as they had for the past few years, because the agricultural economy was not flourishing enough to support them, but they would creep upward. Meanwhile, with farmers facing hard times, custom cutters would be locked into a schedule of rates for cutting that would not change until better times returned for farmers.

All things considered, the signs favored the survival of the business of custom combining as an important force in the agricultural economy of the plains. Custom cutters had fashioned and honed the techniques of management by which they operated during the decades of hard times before the boom of the 1970s. Methods might have become lax and careless during flush times, especially in the overextension of finances, but more trying conditions again would forge them into effective techniques for survival.

Chapter 6
An Unusual
Sort of Life

The harvest of 1947 was a trying one for Alan Ladd, custom cutter. Not only was he in debt to the straw-spreaders, like most custom combiners, but he also faced every trouble that the scriptwriters of Hollywood could imagine. Wheat fires raged out of control. Crewmen staged brannigans with rival outfits. Worst of all was the disruptive influence of Dorothy Lamour, who corrupted crack mechanic Robert Preston into such distressing diversions as marriage and, worse yet, bootlegging farmers' wheat at elevators. It took the powerful fists of Ladd to restore poor Preston to his senses and get the outfit back on the road north. The harvest was filled with adventure, conflict, and wild women in those days—at least as portrayed in the motion picture *Wild Harvest*, by Paramount Pictures.

The harvest in truth had its share of inherent romance, but that was only a part of the lives of custom cutters. *Wild Harvest* and scores of feature articles in newspapers and magazines repeatedly captured the color of the business. Again and again appeared the same photographs of as many as twenty combines attacking fields in close, sawtooth formation—an arrangement practical for photographers, but dusty and dangerous for combines and drivers. In daily life the romance of the harvest was tempered by hard work and weary spirits. "It certainly is not a bed of roses, although a lot of people think that it is," one custom cutter summed it up.[1] Yet if custom combining was not undiluted high adventure, it nevertheless offered its participants a unique style of life little understood by outsiders.

Perhaps the most peculiar aspect of life in the harvest was the social arrangement it created, a blending of the ties of family with the relationships of business. In every outfit there was a ramrod, a boss, or whatever the men chose to call him. Here was a man who played many roles. In most cases he was first of all a husband and father. The presence of his family with him placed responsibilities on the boss that a crew of men did not. If food, accommodations, and cleanliness were not the best, a boss could tell hired men to take it or leave it, but he had to see to the comfort of his family. At the same time, the boss was responsible for a crew of men who needed careful supervision. In other businesses it was possible for an individual to be one man, a gentle father, with his family, and another, a tough taskmaster, with his employees, but for custom cutters family and business were fused. This was especially true when the boss's own sons worked for him. Most custom cutters adopted a paternal attitude toward their workers, although they recognized that too much familiarity could lead to laxness. Rather than treating their sons as hired men, they treated their hired men as sons.

Outsiders expected custom cutters to be tough, profane men. This was generally true of unmarried custom cutters or those who traveled without their families, but custom cutters whose families accompanied them comported themselves differently. In fact, most professional custom cutters were downright soft-spoken. Either they mellowed with the years, or the countless crises of harvesting winnowed out the most excitable ones, leaving only those able to look on plugged cylinders and busted sickles with equilibrium.

Some bosses were exceptions to this principle, for each one had his own style. In custom combining it was not enough to direct workers to the tasks to be done. It took leadership to inspire them to stay at the job after midnight of a sixteen-hour day. Some accomplished this by quiet example, but others did it by creating an atmosphere of awe. Before the advent of two-way radios among custom cutters, this sort of boss needed a powerful set of lungs to shout reprimands across the wheat. A gruff front shown to employees and sons alike helped to dissipate talk of favoritism and even could be a stimulus to esprit de corps.

The role of the outfit's ramrod was that of a patriarch, ruling over household, retainers, and possessions. This pushed the boss's wife into assuming the role of a matriarch as much as she was willing to do so. She was not only wife and mother to her own family but also temporary mother to a crew of young men.

How maternal the wife was to the crew was a function of her personality, the age of the workers, and the conditions of the moment. Almost universally she cooked for the crew. Beyond that, generalizations were hard. When the work was slow, there was a tendency to let the boys go their own way and look after themselves. When the work was hard, when the boys had worked long hours for many days, sympathy got the upper hand. While the men were expected to do their own laundry when there was time, when they were too busy she was likely to make a sweep through the bunkhouse and haul a load of bedclothes to the laundry. Meals became more substantial, and at end of day—some time after midnight— there was likely to be some sort of pastry for a snack. During hard stretches of work, the harvesting wife visited the field more often and stayed longer when delivering meals.

Children of the boss had privileged positions, not in the amount of work expected of them, but in status. Sons were not just workers, they were heirs, expected to assume more and more responsibility in managing the outfit as they grew older. They were more likely to choose their jobs rather than have them assigned. Daughters shaped their roles to suit their preferences. Some chose to operate combines or trucks, others were happy to decline, while still others joined in the field work only when necessary. Young children led a meandering life, seeing a succession of new towns and places, taking the wheel of the combine for a round, moving as they pleased through the masculine society of the harvest.

Among the hired men there developed a set of roles that

Fourth-generation custom cutters Allen Squires and Cindy
Squires worked alongside their parents and crewmen in 1977.

140

Everett Squires, left, clowns beside a stalled truck with two sons, Richard (leaning on the fender) and Ronald (front), in about 1950. Seated on a fender is Paul Mercer, a crewman.
Photo courtesy of Everett and Mable Squires.

was not exactly a pecking order, but that certainly indicated a sense of each man knowing his place. The job of combine driver was a bit more prestigious than that of truck driver. Combine driving took more skill with the controls, and the item of machinery was more vulnerable and more valuable

141

than a truck. Combine drivers liked their job because they were responsible for nothing else except running their machines. Their duties were clear. Some workers preferred to drive a truck for the sake of variety of tasks. Truck driving meant frequent trips to town, or at least to an elevator, and truck drivers also were expected to pitch in on any odd job that had to be done when not actually driving. Combine drivers and truck drivers had to be prepared to trade jobs if necessary. Some bosses made it a practice to rotate jobs, while others just wanted their truck drivers to be able to run a combine for a few minutes while the combine driver ate a meal.

Further specialization also developed, especially in large crews. It soon became known which hands had special skills— knowledge of wiring, expertise in engines, ability to weld, or just a strong arm. From any crew emerged a top hand or two who did more than his share of the work. He was the one who joined in to help whenever there was a breakdown and to whom others turned when the boss was absent and they needed advice. It was possible for a laborer to get by doing only his bare share of the work, but he was soon known to his fellows. Truck drivers, when asked to, willingly pointed out the best combine driver on the crew; combine drivers knew just as well which truck drivers were most reliable.

Foremen were scarce in custom cutting, but a few crews had them. They were hired for one of two reasons. The first was that the boss was retired or easing into retirement and had no son or successor taking over the operation. The foreman in this case either was a junior partner or hoped to become one. The boss then confined his duties to negotiations with customers and matters of finance, as well as making decisions about when to move from one area to another. The foreman supervised the work in the field. The other possible reason for having a foreman was that the outfit was large enough to split up to work on more than one job at once. Then a foreman handled one portion of the outfit, the boss the other. The foreman in either case was expected to be much more than a supervisor. He also was a skilled mechanic, hired as much for that skill as for any other reason.

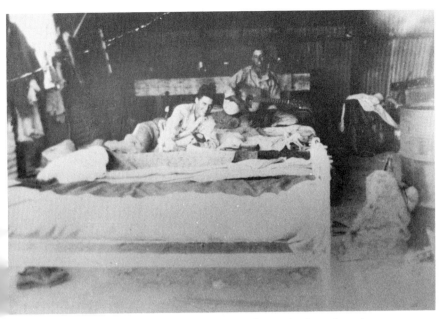

These custom crewmen slept in a round-top shed on the Elmer
Graffis farm, Seibert, Colorado, in 1948.
Photo courtesy of Elmer Graffis.

For all members of the outfit, the quality of life on the road
improved greatly through the years. Housing was an obvious
concern. During the early years of the business few custom
cutters took their families along on the harvest, and the hired
men enjoyed little personal comfort. Of the custom outfits in
Nebraska in 1942, fewer than one in twenty had any sort of
trailer or bus for sleeping. This meant that pioneering custom
cutters relied on local accommodations, and during the harvest, hotels soon filled up. Farmers provided some lodgings,
but too often the harvesters had to shift for themselves, sleeping in their trucks, in granaries, or under tarpaulins. A few
custom cutters carried tents.

Later in the 1940s house trailers became common in custom outfits, for more custom cutters began taking their fam-

ilies along on the harvest. Early house trailers varied greatly in quality. Some were commercially manufactured, while others were homemade frames with aluminum or steel sheeting tacked on. The first house trailers appeared as lodgings for the boss and his family, with crewmen still sleeping wherever there was shelter, but soon custom cutters began to include additional trailers as bunkhouses. During the late 1940s some of these were army-surplus troop carriers. By 1971 most custom outfits had house trailers, and many also had campers or buses for the hired men; 3,431 custom outfits boasted 2,296 house trailers and 793 campers or buses. Many custom cut-

Mable Squires beside the house trailer that was her home on the road in 1950.
Photo courtesy of Everett and Mable Squires.

144

Custom combiners parked their house trailers on a vacant lot in
Taloga, Oklahoma, in 1977.

ters, those with short routes who did not take their families
with them, still relied on local accommodations.[2]

The addition of a house trailer to an outfit did not necessarily make life luxurious. Mable Squires recalled that when
she began making the harvest with her husband, Everett, in
1948, he always parked their trailer in the field, rather than in
town or at the farmyard. This was to keep rowdy crewmen
away from any place where they could find trouble.[3] Mobile
home parks were still a thing of the future in the early days,
and hookups for electricity and plumbing often were unavailable. The proliferation of house trailers among custom cutters
itself raised problems. Trailer parks handled some of the traffic, but parking spaces were at a premium in the tiny towns
frequented by custom combiners. Alleys and vacant lots, fair-
grounds and football fields, even parks and courthouse squares
became haunts for harvesters.

By the 1970s professional custom cutters lived in some
comfort. They established regular parking places for each
year at each stop on the route and reserved their spaces well

in advance. Their trailers were filled with the same conveniences they enjoyed at home—modern kitchens, air conditioning, comfortable beds, and television sets.

A great problem of early custom cutters was obtaining meals substantial enough for men working long hours. Cafes, like hotels, were jammed during harvest, and custom cutters could not afford to wait long to be served. Lines of hungry harvesters stretched out of the doors of diners and into the streets. All too often during World War II cafes closed their doors because they ran out of food, especially meat. Those custom cutters who turned to grocery stores in hopes of cooking for themselves found shortages there also. Everett Squires recalled being desperate enough in such a situation in Tribune, Kansas, during the war that he and his men pursued cows in pastures for milk.[4] Even if enough groceries were available, some member of the crew had to rise early to cook breakfast and retire late after finishing the dishes. The noon meal for early custom cutters was a sandwich eaten on the run. Occasionally there was relief from such difficulties. Women in the towns sometimes opened special kitchens to serve harvesters during the war, much as they did for soldiers. Custom cutters held ample shares of rationing coupons that they turned over to the women serving them.

From the standpoint of nutrition, the addition of a woman to an outfit was a godsend. This meant palatable meals at last, often cooked on kerosene burners or on the ground. Once harvesting wives acquired modern kitchens, they turned out meals probably better and certainly bigger than what the men had at home. The usual practice was to serve breakfast in the trailer and to take a noon meal (dinner, not lunch) and an evening meal (supper, not dinner) to the field. Some bosses insisted that dinner be a smaller meal than the others, lest the largess of the cooks slow their men down on warm, sleepy afternoons. Casseroles figured largely in the menu because of the number of men to be served, but steaks were not unknown, and hamburgers were a staple in dinners carried to the field.

In 1948 the cook of a custom outfit on the Elmer Graffis farm slept
in the tent on the right and served in the one on the left.
Photo courtesy of Elmer Graffis.

Even laundry and bathing were problems for early custom
cutters. Coin-operated laundries were rare in the 1940s in the
areas where custom cutters operated, and cleaners could not
handle the volume of work presented them during harvest.
Clothes therefore were washed only occasionally. Baths were
even rarer occurrences, unless stock tanks were handy.

For some years Mable Squires did the laundry of her husband and all the hired men on a scrubboard, but harvest
hands then and later usually were expected to do their own
washing. The best-hated memories of many hired hands were
of folding laundry in a laundromat after a long day's work in
the field. Laundry usually was a task for rainy days, but sometimes the rainy days were too far between.

147

The Pete Peters outfit ate this meal in the field on the Robert
Means farm, Cherokee, Oklahoma, in 1954.
Photo courtesy of Pete Peters.

With their busy schedule, the social life of custom cutters
was limited during harvest. Of the men of the outfit, the person who had the most contact with outsiders was the boss,
and this consisted almost entirely of business. He negotiated
with farmers, talked with elevator operators, fetched parts
from implement dealers, bought fuel at filling stations, and
exchanged information with fellow custom cutters. His conversations with all these people were brief, unless it was too
wet to cut.

Women and children not engaged in field work drew most
of their acquaintances from the families of other custom cutters and the families of farmers their outfits cut for. In towns
on the high plains, the house trailers of custom cutters formed
villages in the areas where they were accustomed to park,

making social contact convenient. Visits among the women were common in the afternoon, and children had playmates. Also, there were calls to make on the wives of farmers, women who became good friends in the course of many years working for the same people.

Flava Bever of Cedar Vale, Kansas, was the wife of custom cutter Alpha "Hap" Bever. Throughout the 1950s she kept a daily diary recording her activities and travels across Oklahoma, Kansas, Colorado, Nebraska, South Dakota, and North Dakota. Her social schedule, while not refined, nevertheless was full. Rarely did a day go by in which she did not visit some local woman. Usually this was to do some work—washing clothes, plucking chickens, making quilts, canning pickles, and even picking chokecherries and making jelly in South Dakota. Ladies in North Dakota, three states away from her home, arranged a coffee for her on her fiftieth birthday. Her teenage daughter enjoyed swimming, movies, dances, horseback riding, and stock car races at various times on the road. When storms threatened, they took refuge in cellars with farmers' families. Flava Bever reveled in the constant activity. For some other women of the harvest, the social contact expected of them could become a burden. Visiting around by the women was one way that enduring relationships with farm families—customers—were solidified.[5]

The social world of the hired men on a custom crew consisted mostly of each other. They had little opportunity to meet men from other crews except briefly at elevators or sometimes on rainy days. If the weather was bad, they might take in local bars, but usually they found themselves in such small towns that the night life amounted to little and ended early in the evening. The love lives of harvest hands in no way resembled that of Robert Preston in *Wild Harvest*, as was well stated by a hulking bulldogger-turned-truck driver from west Texas. Approaching an elevator in Vernon, Texas, with a truckload of wheat, and spying two girls on the sidewalk, he let go a blast of the air horn, turned, and said, "That's about as close as we get."[6]

The lack of amusement for harvesters seldom was a prob-

Above and on facing page: A spell of rainy weather in Selby, South Dakota, in 1967 gave the men of the Pete Peters crew time for card games and horseshoes.
Photo courtesy of Pete Peters.

lem, for if the weather was good, they had no time for recreation anyway. Footballs, playing cards, and occasional guitars saw the light on idle days. The most interesting aspect of the summer's stint in the harvest was the country itself. Custom cutting was the finest lesson in geography most youths ever had, for it forced them to live and work in a series of locales, not just pass through them. Occasional opportunities arose for sightseeing. The Squires outfit always took one day off to attend the Frontier Days in Cheyenne, Wyoming, the men riding in from western Nebraska in the back of a pickup. Flava Bever found time to visit the Black Hills, the Badlands, the Great Salt Plains of Oklahoma, and the zoo in Garden City, Kansas.[7]

Such diversions were welcome, for the grind of work often

was severe. The first person up and about in the morning was the boss's wife, along with any other woman in the outfit who cooked. She began preparation of breakfast, which, on a working day, was a large meal. In western parts of the plains she had to have breakfast ready by 7:00 or so, for the light dew meant that cutting might start around 9:00. Farther east, harvesters stirred a little later in the morning, for it took time for the wheat to dry out anyway.

Next to rise was the boss himself, waking at the same time as his wife, but taking longer to dress and get out. He made his way through the kitchen, checking on the progress of breakfast, and stepped outside to put on his boots. By then it was time to call the men from the sleeper. The smell of bacon frying was scarcely enough to rouse them, but a knock and a

151

shout were, allowing a few minutes for the words to take effect. Breakfast followed as soon as the men showed up. It was the least hurried meal of the day and the only one at which the entire crew came together to eat.

All this took place in the midst of a trailer park or harvesters' camp in which other outfits were doing the same. Soon the men streamed out of the trailers and piled into pickups and trucks. This was the time for horseplay by young hands if there was to be any, for later everyone was too busy. The trucks took to country roads, while back in the trailer, the women cleared away dishes. As soon as the dishes were washing or done, they began preparing dinner. Morning offered the women little time for relaxation.

Arriving at the field, where the combines and the trucks had stood through the night, the men began the ritual known as "servicing the machines" or else as "gassing up" and "greasing up." Each man took care of the machine he was to operate. Truck drivers checked motor oil, hydraulic oil, water, and tires, and placed water jugs they had filled at the trailer in the truck cabs. Finishing their tasks, they came over to help the combine drivers gas up. Someone drove the pickup with the gas tank to each combine in succession. The combine drivers continued greasing up, leaving no zerk untouched. Sensitive joints, like the one connecting the pitman bar to the sickle, would be greased again later in the day.

If all was ready before the wheat was dry enough to cut, then the men waited for the boss's word to begin cutting. The boss was concerned with the moisture test in the morning. He carried a moisture-testing device with him or else took samples to the elevator for testing. Elevators generally docked for grain testing more than 14 percent moisture, but farmers often said to go ahead and cut if the wheat was less than 16 percent moisture. Usually the boss could tell if the wheat was dry enough to cut without a test, just by chewing a bit of grain or rubbing some out in his hand.

When it was time, the combines cleared their throats with belches of black diesel smoke. They moved forward rapidly, slowing as they neared the wheat, the drivers engaging the

Crewmen of the Bernel Elmore outfit in 1977 gassed up each combine from fuel tanks in the service trucks.

Greasing up was a morning ritual for every custom outfit.

cylinders and reels and lowering the headers to begin work. Truck drivers relaxed for a while. It took some time for the combines to fill their grain tanks. Conversations were struck up on the CB, mainly about conditions of the field and instructions about where to haul the wheat.

When a combine's tank was nearly full, the driver signaled for a truck to come and dump him. This was easily done with a CB, but in earlier times it would have been with flashing lights or waving arms. A truck then left the edge of the field and pulled alongside the moving combine. If the ground was dry, the combine might "dump on the go," pouring the grain from the auger into the bed of the truck moving alongside. The combine driver might instead stop to dump, especially if he needed to get a drink from the water jug or to make some mechanical adjustment. If the field was muddy, then the truck drivers did not try to go to the combines to dump, but waited for the combines to come to the edge of the field.

Several dumps made a truckload ready to go to the elevator. During the last dump the truck driver climbed into the bed of the truck to even out the load of grain with a hand scoop, "leveling it off." Then he began "tarping down," kneeling in the grain at the front of the bed to untie the tarpaulin fixed there and unrolling it to the back, covering the grain. Dropping to earth, he secured the edges of the tarp to hooks or bars on the sideboards with a rope strung through eyeholes on the tarp's edge or with rubber straps with hooks on both ends. Then he got in the truck and roared in low gear across the field to the road. In rural areas where custom cutters operated, the driving of harvesters hauling grain was notorious. Each trip was a race to the elevator before some other trucker claimed the next place in line to dump. Speeds were as fast as loaded trucks would make, and with trucks burdened with more than the legal limit, it was hard to be conscientious about stop signs. The only stop the truck driver wanted to make was on the scales at the elevator or in the line leading to the scales.

At the elevator the driver waited his turn, then wheeled onto the scales. An attendant emerged from the scalehouse,

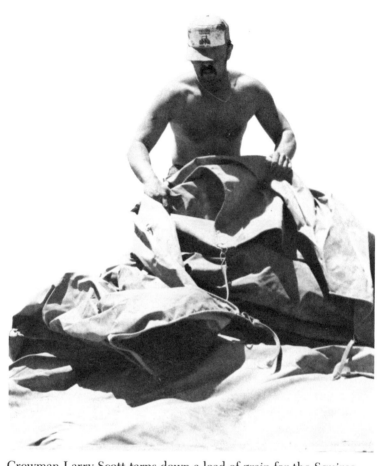

Crewman Larry Scott tarps down a load of grain for the Squires outfit in 1977.

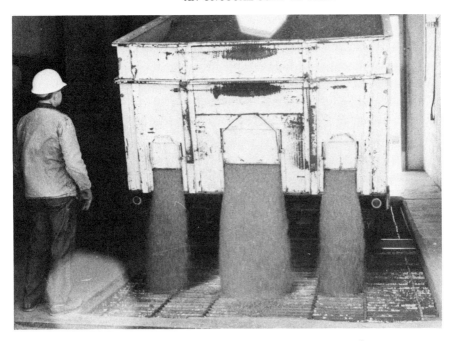

At an elevator west of Tribune, Kansas, in 1977, an attendant watches as grain pours from a custom cutter's truck.

usually a small white building with a large window in the front, and climbed a ladder or platform up to the truck bed. The attendant then took a sample of grain by pushing a probe into the load. The probe took wheat from all depths of the load, supposedly making it difficult to hide wet wheat at the bottom. Using the sample, moisture tests, weight tests, protein tests, and examinations for foreign matter were made. The attendant taking samples might be the grizzled old manager of a branch elevator, but to the delight of young truck drivers, "he" might be a pretty teenage girl—hired, it often was said, to attract trade. The sample taken, the truck rolled off to dump.

The truck entered large doors and stopped over a heavy grate of bars or pipes, through which the grain was dumped.

An attendant, looking like a filthy surgeon with his clothes grimy and his nose covered by a mask, opened the hatch at the rear of the truck and shouted, "Take 'er up!" The wheat cascaded to the pit below. The attendant took a scoop from a corner to usher the last bushels of grain from the back of the bed, closed the hatch, and shouted, "Okay," whereupon the driver returned to the scales. There he picked up a ticket recording the amount of wheat dumped, determined by the weight of the load and the test weight, and the name of the owner. The truck driver dared not lose a ticket. Pocketing it, he sped back to the field with the empty truck. Other truck drivers were repeating the process.

The boss, meanwhile, had a hundred cares. If he drove a combine himself, he issued a steady stream of instructions over the CB. If not, he rushed from place to place. He fetched parts from town. He reassured farmers who came to the field to check on the work ("Yes, sir, I told the boys to run slow and low through that down stuff in the draw."). He picked up handfuls of straw and chaff in the wake of passing combines and inspected it to make sure all were threshing cleanly. He visited other fields to decide where to move next.

Inevitably there were problems, which brought the boss on the run. Usually they were minor: a combine stuck in the mud had to be pulled out backwards, or a cylinder plugged with heavy straw had to be cleared. Other breakdowns took longer to remedy. Worn bearings needed to be replaced, or the welder had to be fired up to mend a cracked reel shaft or some other part. Worst of all, some part that could not be replaced from the local dealer's stock might break. A hundred-mile drive to get parts was commonplace, and implement dealers' parts men, usually willing to help, might fly hundreds of miles to obtain a particular item.

Noon brought no pause in the action. The women delivered dinner to the field, and the men ate—a few at a time seated on trucks or standing. Truck drivers ate quickly and then caught hold of the ladder of a passing combine to drive it for a round while the combine driver ate. Generally, last to eat was the boss.

Crewmen gather around the pick-up as Neva Elmore delivers food to the field near Vernon, Texas, in 1977.

Work intensified during the heat of the afternoon. More people were cutting throughout the area by then, and lines of trucks waiting to dump at the elevator stretched out. The trucks might have trouble keeping up with the combines, and nothing was more frustrating than to have combines sitting in the field with full bins and nowhere to dump. Consulting with the farmer, the boss might decide to haul to some other elevator or to bins on the farm. Trucks hauling to bins on the farm kept up with the combines easily, but truck drivers hated it because they were deprived of their trips to town.

During the heat of the afternoon combine drivers fared better than anyone else, at least in the 1970s. Decades earlier combine driving was a test of endurance, handling clumsy machinery in the hot sun. "If a feller put an umbrella up over

Doug Tony and Allen Squires get their turn at supper in the field before returning to their machines in Colorado in 1977.

Eager to get his machine back into operation, Richard Squires inspects the hasty welding job he has done on a broken reel shaft.

his seat, we figured he was a sissy," one harvester explained.[8] Later, custom cutters overcame these qualms and enjoyed air-conditioned cabs with AM radios. Hydrostatic transmission and power steering made driving less of a burden. Gauges and idiot lights to the right indicated to the driver whether all shafts were turning properly.

If there was leisure for the women with the outfit, it came in the afternoon, after dinner was served and any necessary laundry was done. This also was the time for buying groceries and visiting friends. In the middle of the afternoon began the preparation of supper, the largest meal of the day.

Supper, like dinner, was eaten in the field. This time the work, if it did not stop, at least abated for the meal. The combines might be shut down while the drivers ate, although not usually all at once. The men found seats on vehicles somewhere and ate. When most people were quitting work and going home, they faced long hours yet in the field. They wondered when the boss would decide to knock off for the night. If the wheat stayed dry, they would cut until eleven or midnight, but an early dew might rescue them.

Soon the machines roared again, and as darkness fell, headlights illumined stalks of wheat soon to be swept in by revolving reels. In all directions the lights of other outfits could be seen popping on. In the darkness the throbbing rumble of many combines coming from all directions became more noticeable than it had been in the day. Chatter on the CB died out except for necessary messages. This was the loneliest time of day.

Finally, the word came from the boss to shut down for the night. As each combine filled up for the last time, it wheeled up beside a truck to dump and then proceeded to the edge of the field and parked, taking a place in line with the other machines. The men crowded into trucks for the trip back to the trailers. They retired quickly on their arrival.

Not all days were so grueling. Rainy weather was money lost for custom cutters, but after a long stretch of unabated harvesting, a shower was a blessing to a tired crew. Wet wheat meant sleeping in, breakfast at 8:00 or so, and a day without hectic activity. Men did their laundry and personal shopping. They made repairs that they had been meaning to get around to for some time on equipment. They took combines and vehicles to car washes. Instead of the lonely time in the field after sundown, there was companionship around a card table.

The wheat harvest was a prolonged sprint, lasting from three to six months. During the rest of the year the style of life for custom cutters changed. Crewmen and sons and daughters returned to high school and college. For farming families there was work to catch up on at home. If a custom cutter continued harvesting into the fall, the pace of the work at least changed. If he picked up windrows in the north, his day became shorter because of earlier nightfall. If he harvested row crops in the south, the work probably was near home. The work was not so hurried as the wheat harvest, and so he ceased working on Sundays.

To those not familiar with the business, custom combining seemed like a strain on family life, leading to rootlessness and dissatisfaction. This was not the case at all. No statistics were available, but to all appearances, marriages were strengthened rather than weakened by custom cutting, perhaps because husband and wife both shared in the business. The effect of custom cutting on children of harvesting families seemed to be salutary. Custom cutters never allowed harvesting to interfere with their youngsters' schooling, and about all a child missed out on by going on the harvest was little league baseball. In return, custom cutters testified that working the harvest gave their offspring maturity and industry. Sons of the boss learned early to take responsibility and work hard.

If there was a disruptive influence in family affairs, it was in the area of religion. Roman Catholics and Southern Baptists, Methodists and Mennonites almost to a man joined in the heathen practice of harvesting on Sunday, barring rain. If Sunday happened to be rainy, few harvesters forewent the chance for rest in order to attend church services. If questioned about this, some acted a bit penitent, but not much so, and a few mumbled Biblical allusions to saving the ass that fell into the pit on the Sabbath. Often the women succeeded in packing the children off to church, but rarely the men. Sometimes the farmer an outfit was cutting for wished no work done on his place on Sunday, or in the case of the occasional Seventh Day Adventist, on Saturday. Custom cutters generally then moved onto a neighboring farm for the day's work.

Custom cutters remained mysterious, mistrusted figures to most people not connected with the business. Their image suffered from the preponderance of two related myths about them, the first of which was the myth of the gypsy. Journalists generally characterized custom cutters as footloose nomads wandering the plains. A feature in *Newsweek* in 1977 carried the headline, "Gypsies of the Harvest."[9] Stories of snubs by local people were rife among custom cutters. For instance, there was the family of harvesters that entered a cafe in a small town after nightfall looking as exhausted as they ought to have after a full day of travel, only to be welcomed by a waitress with the comment, "What carnival are y'all with?" Or there was the young harvest hand who managed to make a date with a local girl in North Dakota. As he entered the girl's house, her mother gave him a cold stare and the greeting, "So—you're a combiner." Townspeople on the northern plains tagged custom cutters "wheaties."[10]

Those who considered custom cutters gypsies, migrants, or nomads misunderstood them. Custom cutters never wandered aimlessly, but proceeded methodically from one planned stop to another. They rightly should have been called itinerants, for they had definite itineraries. At each stop there were friendships as well as jobs. Custom cutters often cited as the great joy of their business the string of friends they made on the way north. For a custom cutter to quit the business would have been equivalent to the dweller in a small town moving away from all his friends.

The myth of the gypsy may have originated in associations made early in the history of custom combining. When the industry began, the image of the migrant Okie was still fresh from the 1930s. Many of the early custom cutters were from Oklahoma or the southern plains and thus conjured an unfavorable image as they moved from town to town. People also confused custom cutters with the irresponsible bindle-stiffs of decades past. Such associations became absurd when applied to modern custom cutters, with their large amounts of capital invested in outfits.

A related misconception that also took root in the early history of custom combining was the myth of the ruffian. During the early 1940s, when custom cutters had to hire whatever hands they could find, the workers often were not of the highest character. The business had more than its share of barroom denizens and pool hall loafers not averse to raising hell in quiet towns along their route. Few women traveled with custom outfits, and so custom harvesters were a dirty and profane lot. Everett Squires, a big custom cutter during the war, with his seven machines and twenty or more employees, occasionally resorted to his fists to keep order on the crew.

In a few years the composition of custom crews changed radically. Untrustworthy bosses were culled by economic adversity, and students became the mainstays of the crews. Yet in the towns frequented by a later, quieter generation of custom cutters, a lock-up-your-wives-and-daughters attitude persisted despite the change.

Such impressions differed sharply from the images that custom harvesters held of themselves. Custom cutters considered themselves careful, substantial, successful business-men, and anyone who weathered a number of years in the business had the right to so regard himself. They deplored the denigration of their craft, but while poking fun at the sort of images projected by *Wild Harvest*, they took pride that there was something special and even a bit romantic in their way of life, although they would not use the word "romance." A man with the acumen to succeed in custom cutting could do well in some other, safer business. Why, then, did he follow the harvest?

Most custom cutters answered with a phrase like, "It gets in your blood." They were the first to admit that life in the field often was drudgery and that they were glad when the harvesting season was over, but by the next spring these feelings were forgotten. The difficulty and unpredictability of

165

their business became a point of pride. "It's the exact opposite of going to work at Hesston [farm implement manufacturers]," said Ron Roessler of Buhler. "Every day there is a challenge."[11]

"Custom combining is great. It is a lot of hard work and sometimes a lot of headaches," was the incongruous testimony of another custom cutting couple. "But every spring when the first few warm days roll around, you just start counting the days and minutes until you can head south. It is something that really gets in your blood. It'll be a sad day when we quit the business."[12] For some, at least, custom combining held attractions that far outweighed the toil and trouble.

Chapter 7
Government and
Custom Combining

Custom combining was a business of proud, independent individuals. The man who became a custom cutter showed by that act that he was not one to wait on the beneficence of others, but would try on his own to better his condition. Custom cutters asked few favors of government, and because their numbers were politically insignificant, they expected none. Federal and state governments took few actions for the benefit of custom harvesters, but many governmental measures affected their business. Most of these were actions designed to direct or to regulate the activities of custom cutters.

Early in the history of custom combining, the government of the United States attempted to rationalize the wheat harvest as part of the country's agricultural mobilization for World War II. This was one aspect of an effort to employ agricultural labor and machinery more efficiently when both were at a premium. When the war began, the recruitment and placement of farm labor was in the hands of the United States Employment Service, the organization of which was too decentralized to impose order on the management of agricultural labor. The prerogatives of state directors stood in the way of rapid clearance of workers from one state to another. Reforms instituted in December, 1941, placed more authority in the hands of federal administrators.

The Employment Service supervised the placement of farm labor in 1942, but thereafter, federal administrators and Congress hoped to put such work into the hands of another agency. On January 23, 1943, the War Manpower Administration issued a directive transferring responsibility for farm labor to the Department of Agriculture. On March 13, Secretary of Agriculture Claude R. Wickard assigned the work to the United States Agricultural Extension Service. These shifts only anticipated the formal action of Congress in the Emergency Farm Labor Act of April 29, 1943. This act affirmed the responsibility of the Extension Service, through its state services, for the recruitment and direction of farm labor. The War Food Administration, a division of the Extension Service, was to have general charge of programs for farm labor.

In 1942, the first year of any considerable movement of custom combiners on the plains, they had received little attention from the state employment services. Custom cutters were not farm laborers of the sort that employment officials were used to, and there was no organization ready to handle them. Already in 1942 the Department of Agriculture had stepped in to help with the wheat harvest. Its state and county war boards, part of the War Food Administration, exchanged information about the availability and movements of custom combines, but did little to aid or direct the flow of machines and men. In succeeding years the Extension Service would mount more vigorous efforts.

Under the Emergency Farm Labor Act of 1943, each state extension director was to formulate a plan for the direction of farm labor in his state and then present it to the Federal Extension Service for coordination with other states. Each state extension director appointed a state farm labor supervisor and assigned field assistants to him. The farm labor supervisor set up a farm-labor advisory committee made up of citizens from the state and personnel from the state extension service. The service's county agents were to be the infantry of the effort. Each agent was to establish a placement center for farm labor and set up a farm-labor advisory committee in his own county. He was to solicit the participation of leaders of farmers' organizations, members of the old war boards, employees of the state employment service, and representatives of civic groups. The county agent also was to form a county wage board, composed of himself and four other members, to set wages for farm labor in the county, including rates for custom combining.[1]

The Extension Service was not yet ready to handle harvest labor in all states in 1943, and so many state extension directors chose to farm out the job to the state employment service. The state extension directors who did this made contracts with the employment services of their states to recruit and place agricultural workers. Custom combines were a special case, however. The war boards of the various states and counties had begun the work of planning the movement of custom combines in 1942. In 1943 the Extension Service theoretically delegated this task to them again. The war boards accumulated information about the needs and availability of custom combines, but once the harvest began, they did little. The work of recruiting custom cutters to make the harvest and of placing them on jobs fell into the laps of the county extension agents, the county war boards in many cases specifically delegating all their authority in such matters to the county agents.[2]

The county extension agents, acting on behalf of the county war boards, surveyed their counties before the harvest to determine how many custom combines would be needed and how many owners of combines in the county were willing to do custom work. They reported the needs and resources of their counties to the state extension directors. The state directors in turn made efforts to meet the reported needs in two ways: they called on other state directors and on their own county agents to dispatch combines to areas of need, and they released information to newspapers and radio stations, telling where combines were needed. Fortunately, the harvest of 1943 was not as difficult as that of the following year, and so the Extension Service had a year to tinker with its organization without causing crises.[3]

The effectiveness of placement services in 1943 varied among the individual states, but South Dakota showed how useful such efforts could be. The state extension service stationed employees at Oelrichs and Fairfax, the two ports of en-

Combines harvesting a bumper Oklahoma wheat crop.
Photo courtesy of University of Oklahoma Library.

try through which the most custom cutters entered, and
placed signs at the other five ports directing incoming harvesters to go to the nearest office of a county war board.
Meanwhile, county extension agents had reported their needs
for combines to the state assistant director of extension, who
set up headquarters for the harvest at the office of the state
war board. He telephoned the ports of entry and the county
agents to inform them where to direct incoming combines.
This system gave initial directions to outfits bringing in 253
combines. Other custom cutters entered the state with jobs
already arranged, but received additional work through the
placement service.[4]

Placement generally was more efficient in 1944 than in
1943. The extension services of all the states in which custom
cutters worked except North Dakota discarded agreements
with the state employment services and completed their own
organizations for handling harvest labor, including custom
cutters. This made possible better direction of combines
within and among the states. County agents shed the facade

of cooperation with county war boards and took full control of the program, employing farm labor assistants to help.

A number of states opened special offices as headquarters for the duration of the harvest. These served as clearing-houses for information. In Texas the state extension service set up headquarters for the harvest at Plainview; in Kansas, at Great Bend. In Oklahoma and Nebraska the extension services retained over-all control of placement for the harvest in their state offices, but established area offices in the wheat-producing regions. Clinton and Enid in Oklahoma and Mc-Cook and Alliance in Nebraska were locations of temporary offices. In South Dakota the extension service supervised placement from the state office, but set up a number of area offices. The employment service worked with a similar arrangement in North Dakota. In other states of concern to custom cutters, the extension services deemed their state offices and county agents sufficient to handle the harvest.

In each county the county agents determined how many combines were needed and reported either to area offices or directly to state extension service offices. County agents also maintained lists of farmers seeking harvesters in their counties. The state and area offices relayed to the county agents information about what other areas needed combines. A pamphlet issued by the state extension service of Montana outlined to custom harvesters how to secure placement through the extension services. Custom cutters could obtain information about where combines were in short supply at ports of entry or at county agents' offices. Then they could telephone ahead to the county agent of the county in which they hoped to harvest. When they arrived there, the county agent would direct them to farmers needing cutters. When finished in any county, custom cutters could consult the county agent or the state extension service for information as to where to go next.[5]

In 1945 the extension services expanded their programs for placement further. First, the Federal Extension Service published a map and information sheet for custom cutters. This contained information on how much wheat would be available to cut and when the dates of harvest would be in all parts of the plains. It also provided the names of all county agents. The map showed the principal highways suitable for travel by custom cutters and the ports of entry through which they would pass. The state extension services distributed the map to custom cutters.[6]

In late April representatives from the state extension services concerned with harvest labor gathered in Plainview, Texas, to agree on procedures for clearing custom outfits from one state to another and to compare plans for placement within their states.[7] Each state extension service then in turn implemented its own plan for the harvest. Authorities in Texas fumbled in the face of a difficult harvest. When drought caused abandonment of some acreage in the Panhandle, the extension service issued a statement that the need for custom cutters that year was dubious. Magnification of this announcement by radio and newspapers scared many needed custom cutters away from Texas, causing shortages. Nevertheless, the network for placement in the state, again headed by an office in Plainview, worked well. County agents found jobs for nearly 3,000 custom combines, the majority of which came from within the state, and made more than 2,000 referrals of combines to other counties or states. Despite early problems, more combines worked in the state than ever before.[8]

As custom cutters crossed the Red River into Oklahoma, they saw signs directing them to the nearest county agent's office for help in placement. Early in the spring each county agent had held a meeting of farmers to estimate needs for combines and explain procedures for obtaining harvesters. During the harvest each county agent reported by telegraph to a headquarters established in Clinton, telling of the progress of the harvest and of needs for men and machines. The director of the office at Clinton telephoned the director of farm labor in Stillwater each morning with this information, which was passed on to major radio stations for daily broadcasts. County agents carried out their usual functions of placement and referral. As the harvest progressed into northwest Oklahoma, a second special office at Enid opened for business.[9]

172

The state extension service of Kansas put together a system for direction of the harvest superior to all others. As in other states, each county agent estimated the needs of his county for combines. County agents in counties with the greatest production of wheat hired farm labor assistants and clerks for the harvest. In May officials from the state office held nine meetings with county agents from different parts of the state to plan procedures for the harvest. The state extension service printed 5,000 copies of a guide for custom combiners in Kansas, to be distributed by county agents and at ports of entry.

As custom cutters crossed the border into Kansas, they were registered on forms provided by the state extension service and were referred to county agents for help in placement. County agents in the state placed 2,720 combines on jobs, but this was less important than other aspects of the extension service's effort. County agents were well fitted to keep lists of farmers needing harvesters and to make local arrangements for jobs, but it was unwieldy to have scores of county agents trying to make referrals to other counties at the same time. They could not coordinate their referrals. Officials in Kansas, therefore, placed the job of referral in the hands of the state headquarters for harvest placement. E. H. Leker, assistant farm labor supervisor for the state extension service, opened a special office in Great Bend to direct the harvest. Each night the county agents sent Leker letters detailing the condition of the crop, the progress of the harvest, and the need for combines. Leker charted this information on a map in his office every morning. Looking over the needs in various parts of the state, he wrote news releases for the Associated Press and for the local radio station. Next he fired off a telegram to the state extension office in Manhattan with information for a spot announcement to be carried on radio stations throughout the state. The emphasis of the program had shifted from individual referral to use of mass communication for direction of harvesters. The next year Leker was promoted to regional supervisor of farm labor.[10]

The extension service of Nebraska implemented a plan

much like that of Oklahoma, with two successive centers for the direction of the harvest. The first temporary office was in McCook, on the southern border, and its purpose was to make referrals to counties of need in Nebraska. As the harvest finished up in the state, the headquarters shifted northwest to Alliance, the better to make referrals to states to the north and west.

States farther north generally had placement programs less sophisticated than those to the south. The extension service in South Dakota opened two temporary offices for referral of custom combines, in Pierre and in Rapid City. The extension service of Montana directed placement through its regular state office. In Colorado and Wyoming there was no attempt to direct custom cutters on a state level, but county agents worked locally to bring farmers and custom cutters together.[11]

There were few innovations to make in the system of placement in the years 1946 and 1947 that had not at least been foreshadowed in 1945. In each of the two years representatives of the state extension services convened to discuss their programs for the harvest, meeting in 1946 in Oklahoma and in 1947 in Kansas. Then the states set up their own systems as they wanted them, but they tended to adopt the sort of methods that had been introduced in Kansas in 1945—greater reliance on radio and the press to disseminate information, less emphasis on individual referrals. County agents reported to area or state headquarters daily by telegraph or telephone. By 8:00 or 8:30 in the morning the information was reported to the state office; by 9:00 or 9:30 it was tabulated; by 10:00 or so press releases went out to newspapers and radio. Each afternoon the same information was put into a letter mailed to all county agents. In 1946 the Federal Extension Service again issued a map and information sheet for custom cutters. In 1947 the guide blossomed into a lengthy brochure with maps of specific areas, lists of the names and offices of county agents, estimates of the number of custom cutters that would be needed, and information on the laws of various states in regard to the movement of equipment.[12]

The systems designed by the Federal Extension Service

and its state extension services brought some benefits to custom cutters. It was a great service to a custom combiner just beginning in the business to be provided with customers by county extension agents. The general information about areas in need of combines was of use as well in planning movements. Any benefits that accrued to custom cutters from the efforts of the Extension Service, however, were incidental to the primary purposes of the programs. The task of the Agricultural Extension Service was to please farmers, not custom cutters. The objective was to eliminate shortages of combines and thus save farmers' crops. This often meant the active recruitment of additional harvesters to do custom work, which obviously was contrary to the interests of custom cutters already in the business, for the shorter the supply of combines, the greater the rates they could earn. By recruiting enough combines to serve the needs of farmers in 1947 and earlier years, the Extension Service contributed to the surpluses of combines that prevailed from 1948 on. After 1947 services to direct custom cutters were of less use to farmers, for there were plenty of combines to be had. Accordingly, in 1948 Congress discontinued funding for the handling of farm labor by the Extension Service. Custom cutters were more in need of direction than ever before in 1948, but they never had been supposed to be the beneficiaries of programs for placement.

In 1948 the United States Employment Service again assumed responsibility for the placement of agricultural labor, this time including the direction of custom combines. Thereafter the state employment services, coordinated and financed by the United States Employment Service, administered programs to replace those that had been offered by the state extension services. They followed patterns of organization that the state extension services had developed. The extent of the effort to direct custom combines varied among the states, but the separate efforts had common elements. Each state employment service had a director of farm placement who organized efforts. Each also had a process for gathering and disseminating information about the progress of the harvest. Each state maintained services of placement, compiling lists of farmers needing harvesters and custom cutters needing work.

The system of placement and direction established by the Kansas State Employment Service made good use of the experience of the extension service. Each year the organization published a guide for custom cutters with information about placement services and state statutes. As had the earlier organization, the employment service opened a special office in Great Bend called the Wheat Harvest Control Office. The employment service also had a dozen permanent offices in the western two-thirds of the state, each of which included a farm placement representative. In those counties in which there was no permanent office of the employment service, the service hired temporary farm placement representatives. These often were teachers or retired men. They set up offices wherever space was available, most often in the county courthouse or the offices of the county extension agents.

The task of the Wheat Harvest Control Office was to gather and give out information about the progress of the harvest and the needs for workers and equipment. Each morning the farm placement representatives, both the temporary ones and the ones in permanent offices, surveyed the situation in their own areas. They made telephone calls to elevators to find out how much harvesting was going on, and they checked their own records to see if they had jobs to fill or combines to place. Then they reported by telegraph to the Wheat Harvest Control Office. Personnel there, a supervisor and a couple of secretaries, compiled the information into a daily bulletin that they mailed to all farm placement representatives and distributed to county agents and custom cutters. Then followed news releases to local representatives of the Associated Press and United Press International, which ensured the publication of information about the harvest in newspapers and on radio stations throughout the wheat-producing areas of the state. The dissemination of information by this process was the most important part of the service's work. Farm placement representatives, both temporary and permanent, also made individual placements of custom cutters with farmers. The whole system closely paralleled that which the state extension service had operated earlier, except that farm placement representatives of the employment service replaced county extension agents in the structure.

The system in Kansas changed only slightly through the years. For several years in the early 1960s there was no temporary office in Great Bend, and the director of farm placement supervised programs for the harvest directly from his office in Topeka. In 1967 the office reopened in Great Bend under the name of the Harvest Control Center. There also were two changes in the manner of reporting information to the office in Great Bend. Telephone replaced telegraph as the means of reporting from the local farm placement representatives, and they made their reports to the permanent farm placement representatives in the regional offices of the employment service. The representatives in the permanent offices then forwarded the information to Great Bend.[13]

The Oklahoma Employment Security Commission established a slightly different system for placement in the harvest. The service opened no temporary center for control of the harvest as in Kansas, but directed activities from its farm placement office in Oklahoma City. Like their counterparts in Kansas, officials in Oklahoma used their permanent regional offices, each of which had a farm placement representative, as centers for the direction of combines. They did not attempt to recruit temporary representatives for every county, but instead established from a half-dozen to a dozen temporary offices in areas without permanent offices and staffed them with employees of the employment service. These opened and closed successively from south to north, beginning with one at Frederick on the southern border, and ending with one at Guymon in the Panhandle. During the course of the wheat harvest, the service produced about twenty harvest labor bulletins and issued news releases for newspapers and radio. Placement of harvesters was through either the permanent regional offices or the temporary offices. Like the service in

CUSTOM COMBINING ON THE GREAT PLAINS

Kansas, the Oklahoma Employment Security Commission each year published a guide for custom combiners.[14]

The Nebraska State Employment Service implemented procedures for placement in the harvest similar in some ways to those in Kansas and in other ways to those in Oklahoma. As in Kansas, there were temporary offices staffed with local people in each of the wheat-producing counties. As in Oklahoma, there also were temporary regional offices manned by permanent employees of the employment service, who moved their operations from town to town with the progress of the harvest. Like the other state services, the Nebraska State Employment Service published a guide for custom cutters. The farm placement service in Nebraska also had certain unique features. Before the harvest each year, the service held an organizational meeting at North Platte for all personnel who would be involved in the wheat harvest. The employment service arranged with officials at ports of entry to register all incoming combines. Custom cutters in Nebraska also enjoyed an unusual benefit provided by the farm placement service: the service maintained several camps in which harvesters could park free of charge. The reason for this was that Nebraska almost always had surpluses of custom combines, especially as the harvest entered the northwest part of the state, where the wheat belt narrowed. The purpose of the camps for harvesters was to provide them a place to stay when idle, thus keeping them from cluttering streets and alleys.[15]

The most awesome effort at placement in the harvest was that of the North Dakota State Employment Service. In North Dakota the state employment service had administered programs for harvest labor since before World War II, operating them through 1947 under contract with the state extension service. The farm placement service organized a formidable militia for each harvest—two hundred or more volunteer placement representatives, one in nearly every town. The volunteers were willing to assist not only as a public service, but also because they were businessmen who hoped to attract the trade of people who used their services. Accordingly, the most common place of business for volun-

178

teers was a tavern, with filling stations and grain elevators also well represented. These volunteers performed the functions of placement and intelligence common to the organizations of other states in the wheat belt. Each permanent regional office of the employment service had a supervisor of farm placement who was responsible for oversight of the volunteer farm placement representatives in his area.

Officials of the farm placement office in North Dakota spared no efforts in spreading information about the harvest. They issued daily harvest labor bulletins—"pink sheets"— and press releases to newspapers, radio stations, and news services. They prepared special interviews and radio spots for broadcast before the harvest. They published and distributed a guide for custom cutters.[16]

Other state employment services made less extensive preparations for handling the harvest. The farm placement service of the South Dakota State Employment Service opened only four to six temporary offices each year. The services in Montana, Wyoming, and Colorado all handled the demands of harvest through their permanent regional offices. Each of these states issued harvest labor bulletins, usually two or three times a week. The Texas State Employment Service originally opened temporary offices for the wheat harvest like those in Oklahoma, but by the mid-1960s the service had discontinued all programs for custom cutters except individual placements through permanent regional offices.[17]

The United States Employment Service provided funds for the state services to offer programs of farm placement, but it did little to coordinate the efforts of the individual states. All individual placement was done on a local basis; there was no attempt to refer combines to specific destinations across state lines. From 1959 to 1966 the ten states of the Great Plains maintained an arrangement to exchange information among themselves, but the parties eventually concluded that such a broad agreement was unnecessary. The individual states continued to keep each other informed, mailing their harvest labor bulletins to neighboring states. Only in one year did the United States Employment Service publish a comprehensive guide for custom cutters with information on all the states of the Great Plains.[18]

The programs conducted by the farm placement services of the various states were of more use to some custom cutters than to others. Custom cutters just starting in the business made good use of the guides published by the states and consulted harvest labor bulletins in planning their movements. Some received placements. For experienced custom cutters the placement services had little value. They needed no placements, because their jobs already were arranged with regular customers; they needed no bulletins, because they learned when they were needed at each of their stops through direct contact with their customers.

Both farmers and custom cutters also mistrusted officials of the placement services, fearing they would be forced into accepting harvesters or jobs not to their liking. Ted Hardwick of Saxmon, Kansas, told the story of how he once entered a placement office in southern Kansas and asked if there were any jobs available for custom cutters. The clerk told him there were none, and so he left. An old farmer who had been seated inside followed him out the door and offered him a job. The farmer had feared that if he applied to the farm placement service for cutters, he might be sent a poor outfit and be stuck with it. He therefore sat quietly in the placement office until he saw a custom cutter that suited his tastes.[19]

The first purpose of the farm placement services of the states, as had been the case with the earlier efforts of the extension services, was to fill the needs of farmers for harvesters. The services were state efforts designed to benefit the farmers at home first and custom cutters only incidentally. Custom combines seldom were in short supply. Whenever a farmer asked the placement service to supply him with a custom outfit he got one, but only a few of the custom cutters who asked the help of the placement services received jobs through them. If the harvest proceeded without complications, then the placement services had little to do except to compile and issue information. When rains caused dislocations in the supply of combines, the placement services served well in bringing together farmers who were left without combines when their custom cutters pulled out and small custom outfits who remained in muddy areas to clean up the work.

Other aspects of government besides placement services affected custom cutters. During World War II rationing was a great concern among them, but, fortunately, officials of the Agricultural Extension Service fought for the interests of custom cutters. They persuaded the Office of Price Administration to ration sufficient supplies of gasoline and tires to keep the combines rolling. Custom cutters had high priority among agricultural consumers of such items because their services were vital to numerous farmers.

It was against agencies of state governments that custom cutters had enduring complaints. Each state had its own set of laws of concern to custom cutters. Not only were they different among the states, but also they were enforced with varying strictness from state to state and from year to year. During World War II, because of the shortage of combines, state officials placed few strictures on the activities of custom cutters and even made special exceptions to statutes in order to help them. The governor of Montana ruled by executive proclamation that because of the emergency, the state would not require custom cutters to license their vehicles when entering from out of state. The proclamation, of dubious legality, never was challenged. Likewise, the governor of South Dakota, when so empowered by statute, suspended requirements for custom cutters to buy licenses for their vehicles in South Dakota.[20]

Later, when the supply of combines was adequate, state officials became more hard-nosed. For many years certain states required custom cutters to buy local licenses for all their vehicles before they could work in the states, or even travel in them. In the eyes of custom cutters, Montana and South Dakota were the great offenders in this matter, for as late as 1975 these two states required custom cutters to buy licenses for the full year for all vehicles. In Montana even self-propelled combines had to be licensed. One custom cutter complained that it cost him more than $400.00 to bring his outfit of four combines into Montana in 1967. Custom cutters believed that the lobbying power behind such requirements came from farm implement dealers, who hoped to increase sales by discouraging custom work.

Other states were more lenient. Some, like North Dakota, required that custom cutters purchase licenses for a half-year, while others required no licenses at all. Officials in Kansas specifically exempted custom cutters from requirements of licenses. By the 1970s, most states had made provision for custom cutters to work under temporary permits. This meant purchasing a sticker good for thirty days or some such period at a port of entry. In most states these were temporary hauling permits no different from those issued to any truck coming into the state for a short time, but in Montana and South Dakota, from 1976 on, custom cutters purchased special harvester's permits.

Other regulations, although not so costly, were equally confusing to custom cutters. Before setting out for the season they had to scrutinize the regulations of the states about oversize loads. By the 1950s, nearly all the states required wide load permits for loads wider than nine feet. Custom cutters with combines loaded on trucks also often exceeded height limits. When hauling grain, nearly all custom harvesters violated statutes setting the maximum weight to be hauled by vehicles of their class. Officials in most states winked at these illegal loads, for to enforce the law would have meant protests from farmers who employed custom cutters. Highway patrolmen in South Dakota, however, had the reputation of being sticklers about weight limits, sometimes even watching the scales as trucks came through the elevator. In any state a single patrolman with a stubborn disposition could cause trouble for custom cutters.

For many custom cutters the most exasperating regulations were those designed to prevent the spread of noxious weeds. These required custom cutters to clean their machines of all weeds or seeds before moving from one field to another. This was impossible to enforce, but state inspectors manned the ports of entry and required custom cutters to clean their machines before entering the state. The states of Kansas and Nebraska had the strictest systems for weed inspections. When custom cutters arrived at ports of entry without having cleaned their combines, they were required not only to clean them before proceeding, but also to drive back south across the state line and dump the weeds in the state from which they came. Harvesters complained that the laws were enforced arbitrarily and inconsistently. Records of weed inspections in Nebraska showed that custom cutters had some reason for complaint. The Division of Noxious Weeds in the Nebraska State Department of Agriculture hired temporary employees to conduct inspections at ports of entry. These usually were retired men. Some of these inspectors turned back nearly half of the combines that came to their posts, while others turned back none at all.[21]

None of these regulations ever was so oppressive as to drive custom combiners out of the business, but they were an annoyance. Custom cutters, with their mobile capital and labor, were a fitting adaptation to the physical conditions of the Great Plains, but political jurisdictions cut across geographic divisions. Adaptation to the physical environment brought conflict with the political environment.

Custom combiners owed some debts to the actions of government in the early years of the industry, when the United States Extension Service and the state extension services did what they could to encourage and facilitate custom work. Likewise, the programs of the farm placement services of the state employment services often were of use to custom cutters. Custom combining did not owe its existence to the actions of government, however, nor did it depend on governmental patronage for continued operation. Had the government never instituted any services for guidance and placement of custom cutters, the business would have developed in much the same way. The industry was the product of environmental and economic conditions, not of government planning. In a larger sense, the effect of placement services on custom cutters was irrelevant, because the services were designed to facilitate the harvest and benefit farmers, not to help custom cutters. To do this, state officials adopted methods similar to those of custom cutters: temporary offices, part-time help, and mobile facilities were born of the same needs for flexibility in the harvest that spawned custom cutting. Seasonal farm placement services and custom combining both were parts of the continuing adaptation of the harvest.

Chapter 8
Harvest Hands
Across the Border

Custom combining found its most suitable home on the southern Great Plains of the United States. More custom cutters originated from there than from any other region, and more grain was custom cut there than anywhere else. The extension of custom combining into the northern plains, however, demonstrated that economic advantage could transgress state boundaries to link regions of geographic similarity.

Inasmuch as the Great Plains extended north into western Canada, it was to be expected that custom combining should flourish there, too. The same circumstances that led to the rise of custom combining in the United States spawned a similar movement in Canada. Within the prairie provinces there was room for only limited movement by custom combiners. By means of arrangements between the governments of the United States and Canada, custom cutters from western Canada were enabled to join the flourishing movement from south to north along the wheat belt of the United States. To a lesser extent harvesters from the United States also went into Canada. Although this seemed like a logical and useful development, it became the cause of confusion and protest.

Wheat harvesting had developed in Canada much as it had in the United States. The adoption of the combine began at about the same time in the prairie provinces as in the Dakotas. As in the United States, the seasonal movement of harvest hands into the wheatlands of Canada reached a peak in the mid-1920s with about 45,000 men involved, the number dwindling thereafter due to mechanization and depression.

At the time of World War II, wheat farmers in western Canada still depended on headers, threshers, and bindlestiffs about as much as did farmers in the spring wheat regions of the United States.

Although Canada entered World War II two years before the United States, Canadian wheat farmers suffered no serious shortages of workers and machinery until 1942. In that year the Agricultural Division of the National Selective Service established the Dominion-Provincial Farm Labour Program. Administration of the program on the provincial level was in the hands of the provincial departments of agriculture, each of which designated a supervisor of farm labor and set up a harvest labor committee. The network of officials was similar to that of the extension services in the United States. In order to recruit sufficient numbers of workers, the provincial departments of agriculture paid railway fares for workers from eastern towns and cities to the prairie provinces.[1]

Seasonal movement of custom combine outfits began at the same time. The harvest labor committees of the western provinces lent all possible support to the business, even to the point of subsidization. Owners of combines who wished to do custom work in another area received compensation for the expense of moving machinery. A prospective custom cutter first contracted with a farmer in another area to harvest his crop. Before moving to the place of employment, he filed a claim with the provincial harvest labor committee. The supervisor either would pay the custom cutter thirty cents for every mile he had to move the equipment or would pay freight charges for transporting the machinery by rail or by truck.

In 1944, the Saskatchewan Department of Agriculture paid 150 claims from custom cutters moving machinery within the province, and in 1945, 157 claims totaling nearly $11,000. Most of the money was for mileage, not freight charges. The greatest movement of combines was into an oval-shaped area of wheatlands stretching from Weyburn and Stoughton in southeastern Saskatchewan to Melfort and Tisdale farther north. The heaviest concentration came to the region of

Stoughton; a few units went outside the principal area to the region of Battleford and Maidstone in the northeast. Most of the combines were drag machines, but about one-third were self-propelled. A few of the machines transported were swathers or stationary separators, not combines.[2]

Meanwhile, the governments of the United States and Canada acted to make possible the international movement of harvesters. On June 17, 1942, months before the United States entered the war, the two governments had established the Joint Economic Committees to foster economic cooperation between the two nations. The agricultural subcommittees of these bodies discussed shortages of labor and machinery in agriculture, including the need for more efficient use of wheat harvesting machinery. In February, 1942, the committees recommended to their respective governments that regulations of customs and immigration be suspended in order to permit custom combine outfits to cross the international boundary with the harvest. Prime Minister W. L. Mackenzie King of Canada and President Franklin D. Roosevelt of the United States met in Hyde Park, New York, in April of 1942 to consider measures of increased cooperation during wartime. One product of the conference was an executive arrangement, announced on April 10, designed to facilitate the movement of custom combines.[3]

The arrangement, quoting the Joint Committees, stated the obvious: "The movement of machines within each country has contributed to economies in the use of machines and labor and achieved greater efficiency of agricultural output. The removal of such regulations and restrictions as now impede the movements across the common boundary of both farm machines and the labor associated with them, would further increase their efficient use, thereby contributing to the common war effort."[4]

Bureaucratic inertia prevented any large movement of custom combines from Canada to the United States in 1942. Canadian officials, because harvest in their country did not begin until September, were in no hurry to conclude definite arrangements for international movement of harvesters. They took no action until June 29, when a telegram from the Canadian Department of External Affairs to the United States Department of State indicated willingness to work out procedures. Thomas Wailes, chief of the Canadian Section of the Department of State, conferred with John Stewart of the United States Department of Agriculture's Office of Foreign Agricultural Relations and with a representative of the United States Bureau of Immigration and Naturalization. Stewart's office soon after recommended a definite proposal be made to the Canadian government: custom combiners were to be permitted passage across the border only in units consisting of a combine, a truck and a tractor if necessary, and no more than four men. No passports were required for citizens of the United States entering Canada, and immigration officials in the United States were to waive requirements of passports for Canadians entering the United States, issuing them simple identification cards instead. These terms won the approval of the United States Department of State and the Canadian Department of External Affairs.[5]

The United States Immigration and Naturalization Service first waived provisions of laws prohibiting the importation of contract labor and then secured confirmation from the Department of State that requirements for passports were suspended. The service opened eighteen ports of entry to custom cutters—eight each in Montana and North Dakota, two in Minnesota. Across the border, paired with the ports in the United States, were eighteen Canadian ports of entry—seven in Manitoba, nine in Saskatchewan, and two in Alberta.[6]

The state employment services in the United States and the provincial departments of agriculture in Canada unfolded procedures for directing harvesters that were remarkable for their informality. A custom cutter from the United States wishing to cross the border into Canada reported to the state director of the employment service in North Dakota, Montana, or Minnesota. If the deputy minister of agriculture in the province to which the custom cutter wished to go confirmed that work was available, then the director of the state employment service issued the necessary documents to pass the custom cutter across the border.[7] A custom cutter from Canada wishing to enter the United States went through the same process in reverse by first reporting to his deputy minister of agriculture. The harvesters involved paid no duties and posted no bond. Canadian custom combiners were not to remain more than twenty-nine days in the United States, for they would be needed at home in the fall, but harvesters from the United States in Canada could stay as long as they wished. Customs officials in the United States imposed one ridiculous regulation: they prohibited Canadian custom cutters from using their trucks or tractors to transport combines from one job to another in the United States.[8]

Because the season was so late by the time authorities acted, only two custom outfits from Canada worked in the United States in 1942, with only one combine each, and one of them stayed just two days. Seventeen custom cutters from the United States took eighteen combines into Canada, not counting several who slipped through a port in Montana without being registered. Most of the traffic moved between Montana and Saskatchewan. The majority of the participants also were from Montana, but a few had ranged north from such points as Winfield, Kansas, and Billings, Oklahoma.[9]

In the first year of the combine exchange, numerous harvesters from the United States considered working in Canada. W. W. Dawson, Secretary of the Harvest Labour Committee of the Saskatchewan Department of Agriculture, assured American officials that he could supply any custom cutter who came north with 500 acres to cut at a rate of $2.25 to $3.00 an acre. Dawson estimated that 200 combiners from the United States visited Saskatchewan to scout for work, but nearly all returned south without bringing in their outfits. Weather was the principal reason: heavy rain and early snow discouraged most from even entering Canada and soon drove home those who did. Also, the Americans found the Canadian farmers unwilling to pay the high rates to which they had become accustomed in the United States.[10]

Circumstances similar to those of 1942 again hampered the international movement of combines in 1943. In early June,

John Stewart of the Office of Foreign Agricultural Relations initiated discussions among representatives of the War Food Administration, the Immigration and Naturalization Service, the Department of State, and the Canadian legation to renew and improve arrangements for the exchange of harvesters. The participants agreed substantially on terms, but although the Canadian government subsequently threw no blocks in front of harvesters seeking to enter Canada, certain American officials were less cooperative. William Johnson, Commissioner of Customs, refused direct appeals from Stewart and from other officials to allow Canadian custom cutters in the United States to move their equipment from job to job with their trucks and trailers. He insisted that Canadian harvesters hauling custom combines and crewmen in trailers and trucks would violate laws requiring duties on foreign vehicles transporting merchandise or passengers. Customs inspectors therefore turned back 150 Canadian combine crews attempting to enter the United States. There seemed to be no way to explain the nature of custom combining to Johnson, to convince him that the machines and men transported were tools and employees, not merchandise and passengers.[11]

Other difficulties arose. Officials of the Immigration and Naturalization Service were reluctant to waive such petty regulations as those requiring physical examinations and identification photographs. Not until August 10 could American consuls in Canada announce that the way was clear for Canadian custom cutters to move south, and by then it was too late. At the same time, many farmers in western Canada suffered crop failures. Few American combines entered Canada, for little work was available there. Only eleven custom combines crossed the border from Canada to the United States in 1943; six crossed from the United States to Canada.[12]

For two years attempts to facilitate the international movement of custom cutters had failed. Part of the blame lay with stubborn administrators who resisted change. More telling, though, was the failure of nearly all official parties to understand the possibilities of custom combining. They thought of the combine exchange as a limited movement of a few machines within a few miles of the border, not as a sustained campaign stretching from the southern plains to the prairie provinces. Negotiations in 1943 nevertheless produced progress in developing procedures. American and Canadian officials made the terms of the exchange formal in an agreement. American custom cutters applied to the state war board chairman of North Dakota for certification to enter Canada. He issued them papers that passed them through any port of entry in North Dakota or Montana. Canadian custom cutters received certification from various officials in their provincial departments of agriculture. All employment was arranged by the placement services of the states and provinces. The agreement of 1943 became the basis for negotiations in 1944.[13]

In 1944, representatives of both governments sought to improve on past performances. Officials of the United States Office of Foreign Agricultural Relations were eager to conclude negotiations early in the spring so that Canadian harvesters might help garner a bumper crop on the southern plains. They urged opening the borders to custom cutters by May 1. Their attempts were futile. Not until May 26 did their representatives sit down with people from the Department of State, the Immigration and Naturalization Service, and the Canadian legation to arrange an exchange of custom combines in 1944. This time, and every year thereafter, the combine exchange was authorized by a simple exchange of notes between the United States Department of State and the Canadian Department of External Affairs. No official openly opposed terms of the exchange in 1944, as had some in 1943, but obtaining necessary consents from various agencies delayed opening of ports to Canadian custom cutters until July 7—again too late for Canadians to join in the harvest on the southern plains.[14]

When finally implemented, the terms under which custom cutters crossed the border were liberal. Certification of custom outfits for passage was much the same as in 1943, except that the certifying agent in North Dakota in 1944 was the chairman of the state agricultural conservation committee.

All ports of entry in the wheat belt were opened to custom cutters, and officials on either side of the border aided custom cutters in obtaining rationed supplies. Confusion and tardiness in the procedures, however, kept the movement of combines small again. Twenty-six combines entered the United States from Canada; four entered Canada from the United States.[15]

In 1945, officials finally succeeded in making the exchange of combines work. The Department of State and the Canadian legation exchanged letters in April to authorize the program for 1945. The letters provided for the opening of ports to custom cutters on June 1, early enough for Canadian combiners to go south and enter the harvest in Kansas and even Oklahoma. Regulatory obstacles had been removed the previous year. By late May ambitious Canadian combiners were waiting on the border for clearance into the United States. The provincial departments of agriculture, recognizing that there would be many applicants to go south, designated numerous local officials as competent to certify harvesters for passage across the border.[16]

Although few Americans entered Canada to harvest in 1945, Canadian custom cutters received significant benefits from the arrangement for the first time. No agency kept a comprehensive record of the number of Canadians who went south to harvest, but J. E. Snowball, chief clerk of farm labor in the Saskatchewan Department of Agriculture, made a thorough survey of custom combiners from his province who worked in the United States. He found that of 207 custom combiners issued permits to enter the United States, 151 made the trip. About 485 men were involved in the movement. The Canadians cut an average of 851 acres to each combine in the United States, with an average gross income for combining of more than $3,000 per machine. Including revenue for hauling, the Canadians together earned more than half a million dollars.

Only a few Canadian machines ranged as far south as Texas or Oklahoma, since they could not enter the United States before June 1, but the majority reached Kansas in time to collect bonanza rates, harvesting a fine crop. Most of the Canadians then harvested their way through Nebraska and South Dakota and headed home, skipping over North Dakota and Montana in order to reach their own farms early for harvest.[17]

Canadians making the harvest in the United States reported a host of problems, the greatest of which was rain, which struck them in Kansas and discouraged some before they were well started. Others learned lessons of management from difficulties in 1945. They discovered that for an extended campaign in the harvest, they needed new machinery, for they found it hard to obtain parts for old combines that broke down. Some attempted to ship their equipment to the southern plains by rail and pick it up there, but they ended up spending most of June waiting for their combines. Many mourned the difficulties they had with their hired workers, especially when liquor was involved. The workers knew that their employers had little choice but to keep them on no matter what they did, for they were isolated in the middle of the United States. Custom cutters learned to pick their crewmen more carefully. "They have to be on the job, dependable and non-drinkers," advised one combiner from sad experience. "If one man starts drinking, the rest do the same." The most troublesome problem was that of Joseph Lambrecht, of Ceylon, Saskatchewan. He was held up with his outfit at the border for eight precious days because he was born in Germany.

Despite these difficulties, most Canadian custom cutters exulted over their success in 1945 and looked forward to better years to come. "I consider that we rendered sincere service to these people [farmers in the United States] and they in turn treated us royally and paid us well. Personally I hope a similar arrangement is carried out next year," wrote one. Another added, "It is a very good thing for Canadian farmers. Besides keeping high priced machinery working you learn a lot about the conditions of the American farmer which certainly treat you like a brother." Many indicated that they had arranged to work for the same farmers in 1946, if allowed to come back.[18]

The successful season of 1945 inspired Canadian officials to seek permanent establishment of the exchange of combines. The original arrangement, it was generally understood, had been for the duration of the war. In August, 1945, an under-secretary of external affairs in Ottawa wrote the American ambassador to Canada that his government wished to extend the system indefinitely. For the first time a Canadian official at a high level expressed understanding of the nature of custom harvesting by referring to it as an extended seasonal movement. The writer pointed out the benefits that the United States already had received in 1945 in help with the harvest, but also noted that custom combining was an opportunity for farmers in western Canada experiencing crop failures to supplement meager incomes. "It would be a simple matter to extend these mutual benefits into the postwar period," he concluded.[19]

Accordingly, the next spring the respective governments again exchanged letters to authorize international movement of harvesters. Arrangements were completed early in the spring, and so the Immigration and Naturalization Service admitted custom cutters from Canada as early as May 15. Some 225 combines already had cleared the border by June 5. Altogether, about 460 custom combines entered the United States from Canada in 1946, a great increase over 1945. Three hundred and fifty-eight combines came from Saskatchewan, accompanied by about 1,100 men. Based on the returns of 263 of them, they cut an average of 973 acres to a combine in the United States, for an estimated total of nearly 350,000 acres cut by all units from Saskatchewan. They earned more than a million dollars in the United States for combining alone, not counting charges for hauling. Nearly a third of their work was in Kansas, but they also covered a good deal of acreage in Oklahoma, Nebraska, and South Dakota.[20]

Once again, returning Canadian custom cutters expressed satisfaction with their venture into the United States. "We attempted to make an excellent job so that Canadian machines would be wanted the next season," explained one. "As a result of this we have contracts for 4,000 acres for 1947." "They all want us back again," was the testimony of others. Yet there were dissenters in the ranks whose voices foreshadowed ill feelings that would arise in decades to come. "I would say that no more Canadians should go south," wrote one disillusioned harvester, explaining that although Canadian custom cutters had made a good reputation in the United States, American combiners thereafter should be able to handle their own harvesting.[21]

The movement of combines swelled to its peak in 1947. The Canadian Department of External Affairs once again exchanged notes with the American Embassy in Ottawa to authorize the arrangement. Eager custom combiners from Canada, flushed and impressed by the profits of 1946, clamored for papers to pass them across the border on May 25, the date set for opening ports to custom cutters in 1947. The Farm Labour Division of the Saskatchewan Department of Agriculture demonstrated its willingness to help them by sending its secretary, Roy Fysh, to Kansas to meet with representatives of the state extension services. Fysh, greeted warmly by state extension directors, who hoped to recruit combines from Saskatchewan for their harvest, assured them that Saskatchewan was willing to supply all the combines they wanted.[22]

Canadian custom cutters were only too willing to back up Fysh's pledge. The United States Extension Service first notified Canadian officials that they should certify 300 custom combines to enter the United States. Canadian applicants for certification far exceeded that number, and so officials of the Canadian Department of Agriculture devised a system of quotas, allotting numbers of combines to be certified among the provinces according to the number who had come from each the previous year. More than three-fourths of the machines, therefore, were to come from Saskatchewan, the rest from Alberta and Manitoba. Officials of the Farm Labour Committee in Saskatchewan also devised a point system to decide what individuals should be granted passage, with preference given to veterans of the armed forces, custom cutters who had combined in the United States before, and, most of all, farmers from districts struck by drought.[23]

195

As the harvest progressed into Kansas out of Texas and Oklahoma, where there were sufficient combines in 1947, directors of state extension services in the central plains grew panicky. Combines were in seriously short supply. Bernard Joy, deputy director of the Federal Extension Farm Labor Program, remained calm, for he knew that once the harvest moved past Kansas, demand for combines would decrease. Nevertheless, he said, "reports of probable loss of wheat because of a shortage of combines will be general, and possibly hysterical," and so the Federal Extension Service gave in to pressure to admit more Canadians. They ordered 150 more combines on June 6, 300 on June 16, 150 on June 23, 100 on June 24, and 200 on June 27. Most of the orders were filled by waiting custom cutters, but the last order was so late that few custom cutters still were willing to start south.[24]

Out of a total of about 1,100 combines from Canada, 649 machines from Saskatchewan worked in the United States in 1947. The 649 from Saskatchewan cut an average of 860 acres apiece in the United States, more than half a million acres in all. Once again, about a third of the acres were in Kansas. Earnings of harvesters from Saskatchewan in the United States totaled more than three million dollars for combining and hauling.[25]

The availability of work in the United States and the restrictions on the numbers of combiners allowed to enter tempted some custom cutters to slip across the border illegally. American officials, knowing the need for combines, were reluctant to take action against the offenders. Two men from Saskatchewan, D. A. Graber and V. C. Johnson, took a combine across without a permit and headed for Texas. Worse yet, this was the second year they had done so. Farm labor officials in Saskatchewan learned that Graber and Johnson were harvesting flax near Beeville, Texas, and insisted that federal extension officials see that the two were sent home. Members of the Border Patrol unit at San Antonio accosted the combining culprits in the field. Although the two did not have the papers they should have had from officials in Saskatchewan, they did have identification cards from the United States Immigration and Naturalization Service. The Border Patrol therefore left them to work undisturbed.[26]

The international movement of harvesters had reached its peak in 1947. In succeeding years Canadians continued to come to the United States to harvest, but never again in such numbers. Partly this was the result of the general depression in the custom cutting business starting in 1948, and partly it was because American officials, no longer faced with shortages of combines, did not need to appeal to Canada for harvesters.

The combine exchange continued on its own momentum, however, because Canadian officials wanted their custom cutters to have the chance to work in the United States. In 1948, the United States Employment Service replaced the Extension Service as the agency in charge of the placement of custom cutters. That year the Employment Service unwisely authorized the Saskatchewan Department of Agriculture to certify 800 custom combiners for entry into the United States. No record was kept as to how many actually came, but those that did faced a discouraging season with small demand for their services. In 1949, the Employment Service requested no combines at all. A few special cases were admitted, for instance, a man who had invented a new flexible reel for combines and wanted to test it. In addition, Canadian and American officials worked out procedures for Canadian citizens who owned land in the United States to bring combines across the border to harvest their own crops.[27]

In succeeding years the Canadian and American governments continued to exchange notes authorizing an exchange of combines each year, but the number of combines permitted to enter the United States never was large, and hardly any Americans harvested in Canada.[28] Nevertheless, because throughout this time there was a surplus of custom combines, custom cutters in the United States protested the entrance of any Canadians at all. Canadian combiners no longer were needed to save crops; they were admitted as a courtesy to Canada. Because Canadian combiners were foreigners, American harvesters made them scapegoats for their problems. Americans said that Canadians cut prices below the going rate to secure work. Spring wheat farmers, they said, had nothing to do at home anyway, and so they were willing to stay in the United States and work for lower rates than would Americans. Custom cutters from Canada, enjoying tax exemptions on farm machinery granted by their government, held unfair advantage over American operators. The rumor even spread that Canadian custom cutters were paid subsidies by their government for every acre they cut in the United States.

Except for the rumor about direct subsidies, all the complaints about Canadians voiced by American custom cutters were at least partially true. After 1948, however, the Canadians never were numerous enough to pose a threat to the business of American custom cutters except in isolated, individual cases. Around 1970, when custom combining was at the bottom of a twenty-year depression, American custom cutters began passing around petitions to their congressmen, asking that the admission of Canadian custom cutters be ended. This was the reason that the Economic Research Service of the United States Department of Agriculture embarked on a major study of custom combining in 1971—to see how much of a threat the Canadian operators posed. The researchers found that 116 Canadian outfits worked in the United States in 1971, using 175 combines. The Canadians harvested a total of 435,000 acres of wheat. That acreage constituted only 1.3 percent of the acreage in wheat on the plains, while interstate custom cutters from the United States harvested 31.1 percent. Although there undoubtedly were instances of price-cutting by Canadians in some places, the study concluded that the Canadians were too insignificant to be much of a threat. The study found that the most potent competition to interstate custom combiners came not from Canadians, but from intrastate custom cutters—farmers who combined for their neighbors after finishing their own crops.[29]

The Canadian custom cutters after 1948, then, despite some controversy, were little more than a tiny, colorful addition to the ranks of custom harvesters. The "Canucks" always were an object for comment around grain elevator offices and implement dealerships; a dealer who said that "lots" of them worked in his part of the country usually meant that he had seen several outfits during the time he had been in business. Custom cutters sometimes made fun of the Canadians, who could be recognized, they said, by the insulated caps they wore in Texas in June.

The early history of the exchange of combines between the United States and Canada demonstrated the difficulty of extending an adaptation to a geographical environment across an international border. During the years when custom combining became established in the United States, its advantages in the efficient use of machinery were obvious. Shapers of policy for agriculture, therefore, hoped to extend these advantages to their logical limits, to the northernmost reaches of the wheat belt. It proved difficult because of entrenched bureaucracies. By the time it was accomplished, it was too late; the need had passed. The harvesting season in the United States was long enough to support professional custom cutters within its own borders, and after 1947 they handled the crop with no trouble. Canadian operators came to be viewed as invaders, not as helpers. There were practical limits to the expansion of custom combining, and the international border was one of them.

Chapter 9
The Custom Cutter
Plainsman Nonpareil

In spring of 1944 the initial boom in custom combining was in full swing. Eager opportunists were carving places in the movement, reaping the windfall profits of that time of emergency. Heeding the call of adventure and profit were thousands of ambitious farm boys—among them Irvin Zecha, the son of a Czech immigrant living south of Ellinwood, in central Kansas.[1] In a local newspaper he saw an advertisement for a used combine for sale. He answered the advertisement, but when he arrived at the home of the owner of the combine, the man told him to save his money. According to notice in the day's newspaper, Zecha had been reclassified 1-A by the Selective Service.

Zecha quickly enlisted in the Navy and served two years, but he did not abandon his ambition of becoming a custom cutter. While still in the Navy he sent $800 to his father, asking that he buy him a combine—a twelve-foot, steel-wheeled, chain-driven Gleaner-Baldwin. Returning home in May, 1946, Zecha next purchased a 1934 International truck with no bed and with no glass in it at all, not even headlights or a windshield. He wired a makeshift windshield on the cab and built a grain bed of used lumber. Finally, he bought a 1934 John Deere tractor, also on steel wheels, and fitted it with high-speed sprockets so that it would travel all of six miles an hour.

Thus outfitted, Zecha and his brother, Norman—one of four brothers and four sisters—began custom harvesting near Claflin, Kansas, a few miles from their home. They cut for

200

some days before finishing their first job. Lunch was meager on the final day, for the two were down to their last thirty cents. Then came the first check for cutting, and an infant business was saved.

Thirty years later, in spring of 1976, the second great boom in custom combining was at its peak. Irvin Zecha loaded up his outfit to begin his thirty-first year of custom cutting. He wheeled three twenty-four-foot Gleaner combines onto trailers drawn by two tandem-axle trucks and one bobtail truck. Margaret Zecha, his wife of twenty-nine years, moved their effects into an eight-by-thirty-five house trailer. Four sons and a hired man, after stashing their gear in a second sleeper trailer, climbed into the trucks and headed for Chattanooga, Oklahoma. There Zecha harvested for a farmer he had served for nineteen years. The outfit moved to Wakita, Oklahoma, and cut wheat for a man who had used Zecha for eleven years. The next stop was Great Bend, Kansas, Zecha's home, where he had cut for local farmers since 1946. Ordinarily, the fourth stop would have been Cheyenne Wells, Colorado, where Zecha had combined for a man since 1948, but in 1976 drought had caused a crop failure there. So the outfit moved directly to Oneida, South Dakota, to work on a huge farm with 8,500 acres of winter wheat, the owner of which had employed twenty-one combines the year before. The last stop was Carrington, North Dakota, harvesting for a customer of sixteen years. Finishing the wheat there, most of the family returned home, while Irvin Zecha stayed on with two combines and local help to harvest sunflowers. At length, he also went back to Great Bend, where he harvested a bit of corn in the late fall.

Zecha in 1946 and Zecha in 1976 posed an incongruous pair of images. A shirttail operation held together by baling wire and high hopes evolved into the established business of a substantial capitalist. The wonder of the transformation was not that one individual had succeeded, but that he represented a great class of individuals who made up the business of custom combining. In many ways his experiences were atypical of those of custom cutters as a group, but because of his long tenure in the business, his career demonstrated general trends affecting the industry as a whole. Some of the developments in Zecha's career resulted from personal management, or his own planning, and some derived from events beyond his control.

Success came to Zecha only slowly. For many years he was a part-time harvester, and during the rest of the year he worked at other jobs, such as farming, working in an oilfield, and delivering furniture. The first year, 1946, he and his brother cut only in the Claflin area and did not travel north with the harvest. The next year, after Irvin and Margaret were married in April, and the outfit became a family operation, Zecha expanded his business cautiously. He bought a second combine, another twelve-foot Baldwin, and a second truck, a 1938 Chevrolet, on which he built a bed and mounted a grain blower. The outfit first went on the road in 1947, and from the beginning Margaret Zecha traveled with her husband. They bought a six-by-twenty house trailer with a cloth top. Sleeping quarters were in the back, and in the front Margaret cooked on a Coleman white gas stove. She did the washing with a scrubboard.

Zecha modified his two combines so that they could be operated with a minimum of manpower. He removed the cage on which the combine operator normally sat and lifted the wheels up to the tractor platform, suspended above the ground. The tractor driver then manipulated the combine controls from the tractor seat, eliminating the need for one man. Margaret's brothers filled out the crew in 1947, and she herself drove a truck when needed.

The Zechas began harvesting around Claflin and Great Bend again, and finishing there, they moved on to near Kanorado, Kansas, on the border with Colorado. There they cut for a farm family still living in a three-room sod house with thistles growing on the roof. The crop was heavy, posing another challenge to Zecha's powers of innovation. As grain elevators in the area filled up, he dumped the wheat on the ground. When all the wheat was cut, he removed the auger from one of the combines and used it to deliver the grain to a blower, with which he loaded the trucks to haul the grain to town. Also, the heavy straw was too much for the combines to handle, mainly because the combine controls did not permit quick adjustment of the header height in lodged grain. The rattle chains would not draw the straw through the combines. So Zecha removed the chains and drove nails through the cross-pieces, cutting the nails off as short studs that caught the straw and pulled it through.

The next year, 1948, after cutting at Great Bend, Zecha took the outfit north straight to Oneida, South Dakota. Margaret did not make the trip because she was pregnant with their first child, but Irvin's brother again went, as did his sister and her husband.

The same year Zecha had rented a half-section of ground near Sharon Springs in western Kansas and had planned to put in a crop of winter wheat. Thus he personified two characteristic figures of agriculture on the high plains, the custom cutter and the suitcase farmer, at the same time. Zecha left the crew still cutting at Oneida in the late summer and went to Sharon Springs to prepare the ground for sowing wheat. The results illustrated how important is the personal presence of the boss to the smooth functioning of a harvesting outfit. The night that his brother and brother-in-law finished cutting, they went to Pierre to celebrate. On the way back to camp they ran Zecha's car into a telephone pole, one man landing in the hospital and the other in jail.

The next few years were filled with frustration. In those generally hard times for custom cutters, Zecha kept a toehold in the business, meanwhile working at other jobs and farming part-time in western Kansas. Old machinery had to make do for the time being, but Zecha continued to make one more harvesting stop after finishing cutting at home. Each year after 1949 he cut in the area of Cheyenne Wells, Colorado. He also rented land at Sharon Springs until about 1952, although he never made a good crop.

Once the business had bottomed out, Zecha again began to expand cautiously. In 1952, he purchased his first self-propelled combine, a Massey-Harris 21A, and with the single machine he began an extended route, cutting his way from Chattanooga, Oklahoma, through five other stops to Medicine Lake, Montana. For part of the route he was joined by his wife's uncle and another man, each of whom also had a combine, forming the common arrangement of a working partnership. In order to cut windrowed wheat on the northern end of the route, he bought a pickup header. In the fall he cut milo near Great Bend. Custom cutting grew in importance in his life, and he gave up farming.

Zecha at this point had made the transition from a marginal custom cutter to a professional one. Each year thereafter he harvested a full route. In 1953, he bought the combine that belonged to Margaret's uncle, and in later years he owned as many as five combines. Custom cutting became a way of life, not just a way of making a living.

As a professional custom cutter, Zecha had a basic concern for area of operations. The early process of establishing his route was much like the experience of most custom cutters. He headed for the Red River to begin and found his first job near Chattanooga. From there he followed main routes north to wherever he heard there was cutting available. The northern part of his early route was determined by previous experiences of his working partners, who had established relationships with customers. Once started, Zecha returned to most of the same places each year, modifying the route as it became necessary. The evolution of the harvesting route was less a result of choices or of purposeful arrangements than of circumstances. Experience showed if work was too thin in a particular area or if stops were too close together, and adjustments followed.

One stop each year was at home in the middle of harvest. Others might vary, although certain stops were quite stable, perhaps a key to Zecha's success. In early years, his route tended to be bottom-heavy, that is, he had many stops on the southern plains, often too close together. In 1959, for instance, he worked at Chattanooga, Okarche, and Wakita in Oklahoma before moving to Great Bend (see Figure 13). Few custom cutters would have attempted more than two stops in

Fig. 13. Harvesting route of Irvin Zecha, 1959.

Oklahoma. By the mid-1960s Zecha had spaced his southern stops a bit more, and he found his route more manageable (see Figure 14). His stable route from 1964 to 1966 was well arranged. Stops in winter wheat country were closer together than those in spring wheat country, for the winter wheat harvest moved more quickly. The variety of crops to be harvested in the Dakotas stretched out the harvest there. In the middle of the route was a westward shift from Great Bend to Cheyenne Wells, an example of moving by longitude instead of by latitude to catch up with the harvest. Unlike most custom cutters who made such westward skips, Zecha returned to an eastern route through the Dakotas after going to Colorado.

205

Fig. 14. Harvesting route of Irvin Zecha, 1964–66.

Finally, in 1976, he dropped the stop in Cheyenne Wells, his route thereafter consisting of only five stops (see Figure 15). Earlier ripening strains of wheat in South Dakota, he said, made it wise to move from Great Bend directly to Presho, South Dakota. A crop failure in Cheyenne Wells made it possible to abandon a long-held job there gracefully.

Relations with farmers along the route were informal. There were no written contracts, only verbal agreements. Zecha developed relationships of trust with his customers, who knew that if he was unable to get to a job when expected, it was for good reason. Within this comfortable bond of honor,

Fig. 15. Harvesting route of Irvin Zecha, 1977.

he received rates for cutting that followed closely the general trends in the industry. Figures from his logbook showed clearly the long night of low rates endured by custom harvesters during the 1950s and 1960s (see Table 10).[2]

Through the years Zecha operated from one to five combines, how many depending on several considerations. With more combines he landed larger jobs and did not have to move so often (see Table 11).[3] However, with fewer machines he exercised closer supervision and achieved better efficiency, producing greater profit per combine (see Table 12).[4] Perhaps most important, a smaller outfit could be operated

207

Table 10.

Going Rates for Custom Harvesting,
as Received by Irvin Zecha, 1957–70

Year	Rate
1957	4.00-5-5
1958	3.00-5-5
1959	3.00-5-5
1960	3.50-5-5
1962	3.50-5-5
1964	3.50-5-5
1965	3.50-5-5
1966	3.50-5-5
1967	3.50-5-5
1968	3.50-5-5
1969	3.50-5-5
1970	3.50-5-5

almost entirely by the labor of members of the family, thus saving on wages. Able-bodied sons were an economic asset. What wages Zecha paid to his sons was money that would have been spent for their needs and wants anyway (see Table 13).[5]

In broad strategies of management, such as building a route, finding jobs, dealing with farmers, and choosing how many machines to run, Zecha made judicious decisions. Just as important in his success were other personal attributes, among them inventiveness. Zecha's mechanical skills enabled him to operate used combines for more years without trading them than could most custom cutters, because he reconditioned them himself during the winter. He also modified machinery to suit the need of the moment. Once in the late 1940s, in eastern Colorado, he was cutting wheat so infested with weeds that it would not dry. He therefore removed the cylinder from a combine and converted it into a windrower, with which he swathed the grain and allowed it to dry. As the greatest of his mechanical feats, Zecha once purchased a used Gleaner combine with a twenty-four-foot header, cut two feet off each end of the platform to make a twenty-foot header, and reassembled the platform in smooth working order—a job no professional mechanic would attempt.

Equally important were Zecha's even temperament and dauntless determination. He faced the same frustrations as did other custom cutters. His logbook showed that there were few days in which the cutting proceeded without interruption (see Table 14).[6] Yet he remained immune to temper or panic (except during occasional moments of weakness when dealing with harvest hands too fond of liquor). In 1952, while picking up spring wheat near Langdon, North Dakota, a hired man clogged the cylinder of a combine with straw, so Zecha

Table 11.

Largest Job Cut by Irvin Zecha in the Season, 1955–69

Year	Combines Used	Largest Job (Acres)
1955	2	400
1956	2	238
1957	2	389
1958	3	596
1959	3	657
1960	3	785
1961	3	689
1962	3	523
1964	3	689
1965	3	1,385
1966	4	1,108
1967	4	1,813
1968	4	2,200
1969	4	875

Table 12.

Effect of the Number of Combines on Revenues in Irvin Zecha's Outfit, 1955–71

Year	Combines Used	Gross Revenue (Dollars)	Revenue per Combine
1955	2	10,393.11	5,196.56
1956	2	8,563.27	4,281.64
1957	2	12,944.55	6,472.28
1958	3	15,695.53	5,231.84
1959	3	12,648.34	4,216.11
1960	3	18,534.75	6,178.25
1961	3	11,430.90	3,810.30
1962	3	17,059.85	5,686.62
1964	3	15,841.64	5,280.55
1965	3	20,830.54	6,943.51
1966	4	16,443.71	4,110.93
1967	4	22,397.45	5,599.36
1968	4	27,439.12	6,859.78
1969	4	15,663.07	3,915.77
1971	5	28,375.35	4,963.54

scrambled atop the feeder house to pry the cylinder loose with a bar. The bar slipped, and backward he fell toward the upraised teeth of the pickup header, apparently toward death by impalement. He spun about in the air and lighted with one hand on the header, running a feeder tooth completely through the hand, but pivoting on it to land safely on the ground. He immediately climbed onto the combine again, only to return to the ground, sit down on the running board of a pickup truck, and slump to the stubble in a faint. Revived, and finding the combine still not back in operation, he ascended the feeder box once more, climbed down, and fainted again. "I can't stand the sight of blood or nothin' like that anyway," he later explained. The incident merited only seven

Table 13.

Wages Paid by Irvin Zecha, 1956–71

Year	Total Wages Paid (Dollars)	Dollars Paid to Family
1956	1,896.00	
1958	2,308.35	
1959	3,485.12	
1960	3,442.60	
1961	2,474.90	
1962	3,573.55	
1964	2,539.20	425.00
1965	2,556.90	
1966	3,697.70	893.10
1967	2,995.21	
1968	4,858.36	1,168.80
1969	4,726.43	805.00
1970	5,140.81	1,725.80
1971	6,715.93	1,250.00

Table 14.

Working Days for Irvin Zecha's Outfit in 1955, 1962, and 1971

	1955	1962	1971
Cutting Days	51	56	54
Partial Cutting Days	11	13	9
Traveling Days	21	18	19
Idle Days	37	41	39
Total Days on Harvest	120	128	121

words in his daily logbook—"Ran a pickup finger through my hand."

The harvesting exploits of Irvin Zecha showed that personal attributes were important in his career. From a broader perspective, however, like all custom cutters, he played a role designated him by the geography of the Great Plains. Historians and geographers of the Great Plains traditionally have emphasized the effects of environment on human activity. If Walter P. Webb, author of *The Great Plains*, were to have met Irvin Zecha, he would have pronounced him the archetypal plainsman, the ultimate in adaptation to the geography of his region. It was Webb who pointed out the virtues of mobility for survival on the plains. As examples of mobility, custom cutters make Webb's treasured Texas Rangers look like pikers.[7]

James C. Malin, who wrote *Winter Wheat in the Golden Belt of Kansas*, refined Webb's ideas and applied them to the history of agriculture in central Kansas. Malin shrewdly identified the tendency of farmers in Kansas to abandon the binder in favor of the header as a response to environmental pressures, and he would have viewed custom combining in the same light. Leslie Hewes, author of *The Suitcase Farming Frontier*, would point out strong similarities between suitcase farming and custom combining, two related agricultural institutions of the high plains. Both are concerned with an influx of temporary capital from another locality to impart flexibility in agricultural methods.[8]

Most of all, the broad-ranging sociologist Karl Kraenzel would recognize in custom cutters qualities that he deemed essential for life on the Great Plains. In his innovative study, *The Great Plains in Transition*, Kraenzel specified that survival on the plains required some combination of mobility, flexibility, and reserves, two of which qualities custom cutters exemplify.[9] Custom cutters display peculiar mobility in that they transport the sort of heavy capital usually considered immobile. They also have flexibility: Zecha, for instance, shifted his area of operations as new conditions made it necessary.

Custom combining even permits more flexibility to farmers by freeing them from a large capital investment in harvesting machinery. Custom cutters richly deserve designation as "plainsmen nonpareil," not only because they spend their working lives ranging the Great Plains, but also because they represent the characteristic features of life in the region.

Notes

CHAPTER 1

1. James C. Malin, *Winter Wheat in the Golden Belt of Kansas: A Study in Adaptation to Subhumid Geographical Environment* (reprint, New York: Octagon Books, 1973), passim.

2. F. M. Redpath, "Cradle to Combine," typescript, Kansas State Historical Society Library, Topeka, Kansas, p. 1; Sadie Summers, "Memoirs of John Bell Porter," typescript of interview, August 4, 1936, Panhandle-Plains Historical Museum, Canyon, Texas, p. 7.

3. Merritt Finley Miller, *The Evolution of Reaping Machines*, Office of Experiment Stations Bulletin 103, United States Department of Agriculture, pp. 34–37.

4. Malin, *Winter Wheat in the Golden Belt of Kansas*, pp. 62–65.

5. Miller, *Evolution of Reaping Machines*, pp. 37–39; J. H. Arnold, "Farm Practices in Growing Wheat," *Yearbook of the United States Department of Agriculture, 1919* (Washington, D.C.: Government Printing Office, 1920), pp. 137–38.

6. Arnold P. Yerkes and L. M. Church, *Cost of Harvesting Wheat by Different Methods*, United States Department of Agriculture Bulletin 627, pp. 3, 15; Arnold, "Farm Practices in Growing Wheat," pp. 137–38, 143–44.

7. Lillian Church, *Partial History of the Development of Grain Threshing Implements*, Information Series 73, Bureau of Agricultural Engineering, passim; Redpath, "Cradle to Combine," pp. 6–7; Summers, "Memoirs of John Bell Porter," p. 3; George D. Harper, "Eighty Years of Recollections," typescript, Panhandle-Plains Historical Museum, p. 3; Archie Acker, "Memoirs of L. A.

Pierce," transcript of interview, August 3, 1936, Panhandle-Plains Historical Museum, pp. 5–6.

8. J. C. Rundles, "The Thrashing Ring in the Corn Belt," *Yearbook of the United States Department of Agriculture, 1918* (Washington, D.C.: Government Printing Office, 1919), pp. 247–68.

9. Personal interview with Floyd Bever, Sedan, Kansas, April 13, 1976; E. L. Currier, *The Cost of Growing Wheat in Typical Nonirrigated Areas in Montana*, Montana Agricultural Experiment Station Bulletin 122, p. 159.

10. Paul S. Taylor, "Migratory Laborers in the Wheat Belt: Second Half of Nineteenth Century," typescript produced by University of California at Davis, 1957, passim; Don D. Lescohier, *Harvest Labor Problems in the Wheat Belt*, United States Department of Agriculture Bulletin 1020, passim; Don D. Lescohier, *Sources of Supply and Conditions of Employment of Harvest Labor in the Wheat Belt*, United States Department of Agriculture Bulletin 1211, passim; Don D. Lescohier, *Conditions Affecting the Demand for Harvest Labor in the Wheat Belt*, United States Department of Agriculture Bulletin 1230, passim.

11. F. Hal Higgins, "The Moore-Hascall Harvester Centennial Approaches," *Michigan History*, Vol. 14, No. 3 (July, 1930), pp. 415–37; F. Hal Higgins, "John M. Horner and the Development of the Combined Harvester," *Agricultural History*, Vol. 32, No. 1 (January, 1958), pp. 14–17.

12. Higgins, "John M. Horner and the Development of the Combined Harvester," pp. 19–24; F. Hal Higgins, "The Cradle of the Combine," *Pacific Rural Press*, Vol. 133, No. 8 (February 20, 1937), pp. 284–85.

13. *Great Bend Tribune*, July 26, 1937, typescript in clippings collections, Kansas State Historical Society Library; *Larned Chronoscope*, July 8, 1937, typescript in ibid.

14. Evan A. Hardy, "Combines, Old and New," *Nor'West Farmer*, May 21, 1928, p. 7; "Early Combines in Saskatchewan," typescript of clippings, Saskatchewan Archives Office, Regina, Saskatchewan; Lewis H. Thomas, "Early Combines in Saskatchewan," *Saskatchewan History*, Vol. 8, No. 1 (Winter, 1955), pp. 1–2; A. E. Starch and R. M. Merrill, *The Combined Harvester-Thresher in Montana*, Montana Agricultural Experiment Station Bulletin 230, p. 6.

15. L. A. Reynoldson, R. S. Kifer, J. H. Martin, and W. R. Humphries, *The Combined Harvester-Thresher in the Great*

Plains, United States Department of Agriculture Bulletin 70, pp. 2–3.

16. H. B. Walker and E. L. Rhodes, "The Combine Harvester in Kansas," *Wheat in Kansas: Report of the Kansas State Board of Agriculture for the Quarter Ending September, 1920,* p. 273; Edwin A. Hunger, "Kansas Outstanding Leader in the Use of the Combine," *Twenty-seventh Biennial Report of the Kansas State Board of Agriculture,* 1930, p. 187.

17. H. P. Smith and Robert P. Spilman, *Harvesting Grain with the Combined Harvester-Thresher in Northwest Texas,* Texas Agricultural Experiment Station Bulletin 373, p. 5; J. O. Ellsworth and R. W. Baird, *The Combine Harvester on Oklahoma Farms, 1926,* Oklahoma Agricultural Experiment Station Bulletin 162, p. 3.

18. Reynoldson, et al., *Combined Harvester-Thresher in the Great Plains,* passim.

19. Ibid., pp. 52–57; L. C. Aicher, "Problems of the Combine Harvester," *Report of the Kansas State Board of Agriculture for the Quarter Ending March, 1930,* pp. 101–107.

20. Hiram M. Drache, *Beyond the Furrow: Some Keys to Successful Farming in the Twentieth Century* (Danville, Illinois: Interstate Printers and Publishers, 1976), pp. 116–18; Starch and Merrill, *Combined Harvester-Thresher in Montana,* pp. 6–7.

21. Alva H. Benton, R. H. Black, W. R. Humphries, W. M. Hurst, C. E. Mangels, R. C. Miller, L. A. Reynoldson, H. E. Shielstad, and T. E. Stoa, *The Combined Harvester-Thresher in North Dakota,* North Dakota Agricultural Experiment Station Bulletin 225, pp. 4–17; R. C. Miller, "The Combine in North Dakota," *Agricultural Engineering,* Vol. 7, No. 5 (May, 1927), pp. 115–16; Gabriel Lundy, L. H. Klages, and J. F. Goss, *The Use of the Combine in South Dakota,* South Dakota Agricultural Experiment Station Bulletin 244, pp. 5–7, 55–57.

22. Starch and Merrill, *Combined Harvester-Thresher in Montana,* pp. 32–38; "Operating a 95,000-Acre Wheat Farm," *Mechanical Engineering,* Vol. 50, No. 10 (October, 1928), pp. 750–51; D. E. Wiant and R. L. Patty, *Combining Grain in Weed-free Fields,* South Dakota Agricultural Experiment Station Bulletin 251, pp. 3–11; H. F. McColly, "The Combine in the Spring Wheat Area," *American Thresherman,* May, 1931, pp. 8–9; A. J. Schwantes, "Windrow Method of Combine Harvesting," *Agricultural Engineering,* Vol. 10, No. 2 (February, 1929), pp. 49–50; I. D. Mayer, "Windrow and Pick-up Attachments," *Agricultural Engineering,* Vol. 10, No. 2

(February, 1929), pp. 67–68; J. K. Mackenzie, "The Windrow Harvester," *American Thresherman*, May, 1931, pp. 5, 18.

23. Lundy, et al., *Use of the Combine in South Dakota*, pp. 4–5; Benton, et al., *Combined Harvester-Thresher in North Dakota*, pp. 3–4.

24. J. G. Taggart and J. K. Mackenzie, *Seven Years' Experience with the Combined Reaper-Thresher*, Dominion of Canada Department of Agriculture Bulletin 118, passim; Evan A. Hardy, "The Combine Harvester in Western Canada," *Scientific Agriculture*, Vol. 12, No. 3 (November, 1931), pp. 121–28; Evan A. Hardy, "The Combine in Canada," *American Thresherman*, May, 1931, pp. 9, 17; Evan A. Hardy, "The Combine in the Prairie Provinces," *Agricultural Engineering*, Vol. 10, No. 2 (February, 1929), pp. 55–56; Evan A. Hardy, "The 'Combine' in Saskatchewan," *Agricultural Engineering*, Vol. 8, No. 8 (August, 1927), pp. 206–208.

25. Hardy, "Combine Harvester in Western Canada," pp. 126–27; *The Header Barge Method of Harvesting*, Alberta Agricultural Extension Circular 14, passim; Gabriel Lundy, *The Header Stack-Barge for Harvesting*, Special Extension Circular 7, South Dakota Extension Service, passim.

26. Robert M. Cullum, Josiah C. Folsom, and Donald G. Hay, *Men and Machines in the North Dakota Harvest* (Washington, D.C.: Bureau of Agricultural Economics, 1942), pp. 8, 12–14; Robert M. Cullum, Josiah C. Folsom, and Donald G. Hay, *Men and Machines in the North Dakota Harvest (Statistical Supplement)* (Washington, D.C.: Bureau of Agricultural Economics, 1942), pp. 2–4, 9, 12, 30, 35; Henry J. Allen, "The New Harvest Hand," *American Review of Reviews*, Vol. 76, No. 3 (September, 1927), pp. 279–80.

27. Reynoldson, et al., *Combined Harvester-Thresher in the Great Plains*, p. 57; W. E. Grimes, R. S. Kifer, and J. A. Hodges, *The Effect of the Combined Harvester-Thresher on Farm Organization in Southwestern Kansas and Northwestern Oklahoma*, Kansas Agricultural Experiment Station Circular 142, passim; W. E. Grimes, "The Effect of the Combined Harvester-Thresher on Farming in a Wheat Growing Region," *Scientific Agriculture*, Vol. 9, No. 12 (August, 1929), pp. 773–82.

28. Taggart and Mackenzie, *Seven Years' Experience with the Combined Reaper-Thresher*, pp. 21–22.

29. Reynoldson, et al., *Combined Harvester-Thresher in the Great Plains*, pp. 35–36.

NOTES

30. Smith and Spilman, *Harvesting Grain with the Combined Harvester-Thresher in Northwest Texas*, p. 19.

31. Ellsworth and Baird, *Combine Harvester on Oklahoma Farms, 1926*, p. 6; Starch and Merrill, *Combined Harvester-Thresher in Montana*, pp. 23–25.

32. C. W. Mullen, "Custom Combines," *Power Farming*, Vol. 37, No. 4 (April, 1928), p. 8.

33. Personal interview with Levi Quig, Great Bend, Kansas, March 16, 1977.

34. Personal interview with Charles Hildebrand, Vici, Oklahoma, March 7, 1977.

35. Personal interview with Levi Quig; "Combines Follow Harvest," *Capper's Farmer*, Vol. 55, No. 5 (May, 1944), p. 23.

36. Personal interview with Joe Habiger, Bushton, Kansas, March 15, 1977.

37. Personal interview with Everett and Mable Squires, Taloga, Oklahoma, June 10–11, 13, 1977.

38. Cullum, et al., *Men and Machines in the North Dakota Harvest*, p. 17.

CHAPTER 2

1. Claude R. Wickard, "Wheat Farming in Wartime," *Vital Speeches of the Day*, Vol. 8, No. 15 (May 15, 1942), p. 474.

2. "Wheat Bonanza," *Business Week*, No. 615 (June 14, 1941), pp. 70–71.

3. "Homeless Wheat," *Business Week*, No. 660 (April 25, 1942), p. 81; Wickard, "Wheat Farming in Wartime," pp. 475–76.

4. "Wheat Outlook," *Agricultural Situation*, Vol. 27, No. 7 (July, 1943), pp. 18–19.

5. "West," *Agricultural Situation*, Vol. 27, No. 10 (October, 1943), pp. 18–19.

6. "Rotary 'Shock Troops' to the Rescue," *Rotarian*, Vol. 41, No. 4 (October, 1942), pp. 23–24; "We Did It Before," *Country Gentleman*, Vol. 113, No. 5 (May, 1943), pp. 20, 64; *New York Times*, July 16, 1944, sec. 4, p. 7.

7. "Farm Equipment Available in 1944," *Agricultural Situation*, Vol. 27, No. 2 (February, 1944), pp. 15–16; "Farm Machinery in Wartime," *Agricultural Situation*, Vol. 29, No. 6 (June, 1945), pp. 14–17; Walter W. Wilcox, *The Farmer in the Second World War* (Ames: Iowa State College Press, 1947), pp. 54–56; Bureau of the

Census, *Manufacture and Sale of Farm Equipment and Related Products, 1942* (Washington, D.C.: Government Printing Office, 1943), p. 3; Bureau of the Census, *Production and Sales of Farm Machines and Equipment, 1944* (Washington, D.C.: Government Printing Office, 1945), Table 9.

8. W. S. Johannsen, "The Great Migration," *Implement and Tractor*, July 31, 1943, pp. 10–12, 23.

9. Bureau of the Census, *Production and Sales of Farm Machines and Equipment, 1944*, Table 9.

10. Personal interview with Levi Quig; "Combines Follow Harvest," p. 23; personal interview with Joe Habiger.

11. Personal interview with Everett Squires.

12. Reuben W. Hecht, *Transient Combine-Harvester-Threshers in the Great Plains, 1942* (Washington, D.C.: Bureau of Agricultural Economics, 1942), copy in File 56078/591, Immigration and Naturalization Service, Washington, D.C. Information in Figures 1 and 2 came from tables in Hecht and in E. H. Leker, *Farm Labor Program for Wheat and Other Small Grain Harvest in the Great Plains States, 1943 to 1947* (Washington, D.C.: Agricultural Extension Service, 1948).

13. Leker, *Farm Labor Program for Wheat and Other Small Grain Harvest in the Great Plains States, 1943 to 1947*, pp. 23–25.

14. Ibid., p. 25. Information in Figure 3 came from tables in the same source.

15. Ibid., p. 27. Information in Figure 4 came from tables in the same source.

16. Ibid., p. 26. Table 1 was adapted from the same source.

17. Ibid., p. 28; *Topeka Journal*, May 18, 1948, copy in clippings collections, Kansas State Historical Society Library; Arthur H. Carhart, "Hammtown—U. S. A.," *Rotarian*, Vol. 75, No. 1 (July, 1949), pp. 17–20.

18. *Preliminary Survey of Major Areas Requiring Outside Agricultural Labor*, Extension Farm Labor Circular 38, Agricultural Extension Service, p. 123.

19. Ibid., pp. 128–29.

20. Personal interview with Ted Hardwick, Saxmon, Kansas, March 16, 1977.

21. Personal interview with W. H. Ring, Sedgwick, Kansas, October 14, 1976.

22. C. P. Streeter, "Here Come the Combines," *Farm Journal*, Vol. 71, No. 8 (August, 1947), p. 21.

23. Personal interview with Joe Vater, Enid, Oklahoma, December 15, 1976.

24. Tom Carroll, "Basic Requirements in the Design and Development of the Self-propelled Combine," *Agricultural Engineering*, Vol. 29, No. 3 (March, 1948), p. 101; Merrill Denison, *Harvest Triumphant: The Story of Massey-Harris* (New York: Dodd, Mead, and Co., 1949), pp. 308–9.

25. Denison, *Harvest Triumphant*, pp. 314–15; "An Extra Million Acre Harvest," *Farm Implement News*, March 30, 1944, pp. 26–27; "Harvest Brigade," *Time*, Vol. 44, No. 5 (July 31, 1944), p. 79; *Massey-Harris Self-propelled Harvest Brigade* (Toronto: Massey-Harris Co., n.d.), copy in library of Massey-Ferguson Co., Ltd., Toronto, Ontario.

26. "Massey-Harris Forms Self-propelled Combine Brigade to Harvest 1944 Crops," *Implement Record*, April, 1944, copy in clippings collections, John Deere Co. Archives, Moline, Illinois; *Massey-Harris Self-propelled Harvest Brigade*.

27. *The American Press Salutes the Harvest Brigade* (Toronto: Massey-Harris Co., n.d.), copy in library of Massey-Ferguson Co., Ltd.; *Massey-Harris Self-propelled Harvest Brigade*; "Harvesting Race: Massey-Harris Spots Its Self-propelled Combines in Areas of Acute Machine Shortage, Offers Prizes for Best Performance," *Business Week*, No. 764 (April 22, 1944), p. 26; personal interview with Henry Oldham, Blackwell, Oklahoma, December 15, 1976.

28. *Massey-Harris Self-propelled Harvest Brigade*.

29. Ibid.

30. Ibid.; Denison, *Harvest Triumphant*, p. 316; personal interview with Henry Oldham; "Flying Harvest Hand," *Business Week*, No. 775 (July 8, 1944), p. 48.

31. Denison, *Harvest Triumphant*, pp. 316–17; *American Press Salutes the Harvest Brigade*; personal interview with Henry Oldham; Joe Tucker, "The Self-propelled Combine," *Agricultural Engineering*, Vol. 25, No. 9 (September, 1944), pp. 334–35.

CHAPTER 3

1. Tucker, "Self-propelled Combine," p. 334.

2. John Lewis Fischer, "Custom Wheat Harvesting in the Economy of Western Oklahoma," Master of Science thesis, Oklahoma Agricultural and Mechanical College, 1949, p. 12.

3. Nebraska State Employment Service, *Post-Season Farm La-*

bor Report, 1948, pp. 9–10. Information in Table 2 was drawn from this and successive farm labor reports by the Nebraska State Employment Service.

4. North Dakota State Employment Service, *North Dakota Harvest Labor Report*, 1948, pp. 5–6, and appended farm labor bulletins.

5. Robert B. Gilkison, "Wheat Harvest Pattern," *Employment Security Review*, Vol. 17, No. 3 (March, 1950), p. 30; Nebraska State Employment Service, *Post-Season Agricultural and Food Processing Report for State of Nebraska, 1949*, p. 6; North Dakota State Employment Service, *North Dakota Harvest Labor Report*, 1949, pp. 8–9, and appended farm labor bulletins. Information in Table 3 was drawn from tables in this and successive harvest labor reports by the North Dakota State Employment Service.

6. Nebraska State Employment Service, *Post-Season Agricultural and Food Processing Report for State of Nebraska*, 1950, p. 3, 1951, p. 3; North Dakota State Employment Service, *North Dakota Farm Labor Report*, 1950, pp. 5–6, and appended farm labor bulletins, 1951, pp. 15–18, and appended farm labor bulletins.

7. Charles M. Williams, "Enterprise on the Prairies," *Harvard Business Review*, Vol. 31, No. 2 (March-April, 1953), pp. 101–2; Nebraska State Employment Service, *Post-Season Agricultural and Food Processing Report*, 1952, p. 4; North Dakota State Employment Service, *North Dakota Farm Labor Report*, 1952, p. 10, and appended farm labor bulletins.

8. Nebraska State Employment Service, *Annual Agricultural and Food Processing Report*, 1953, pp. 2–3, 6, 1954, pp. 3, 6.

9. Oklahoma Employment Security Commission, *Oklahoma's Farm Labor Report*, 1957, p. 3; Nebraska State Employment Service, *Annual Agricultural and Food Processing Report*, 1957, pp. 5, 10; Montana State Employment Service, *Farm Labor Report*, 1957, p. 4.

10. Oklahoma Employment Security Commission, *Farm Labor Report*, 1958, pp. 4–5; Nebraska State Employment Service, *Annual Agricultural and Food Processing Report*, 1958, p. 4, 1959, p. 3.

11. Personal interview with Russell Snell, Ellinwood, Kansas, March 13, 1977.

12. Personal interview with Jack and Jan Schlessiger, Claflin, Kansas, March 17, 1977.

13. "Harvesting Corn by Combine," a symposium of papers, *Ag-*

ricultural Engineering, Vol. 36, No. 12 (December, 1955), pp. 791–802; George E. Pickard, *Combining, Drying, and Storing of Corn* (Moline: John Deere, Inc., n.d.), copy in John Deere Co. archives.

14. Registers of custom combines inspected at ports of entry, 1969, Noxious Weeds Division, Bureau of Plant Industry, Nebraska State Department of Agriculture. These registers were destroyed when the Department of Agriculture moved its offices in 1977. The only copies extant are photocopies in possession of the author. Information in Figure 5 was compiled from these registers. Some items of information are missing or illegible, and so the number of units considered in various parts of this study is not always equal to the total number of combine entries in the registers.

15. South Dakota Non-Resident Custom Combiners Permits, Division of Motor Vehicles, South Dakota Department of Public Safety, Pierre, South Dakota. Information in Figure 6 was compiled from these permits.

16. Permits issued to custom combiners in Montana, 1976, Montana Department of Highways, Helena, Montana. Data from the permits were incorporated into a report compiled for a client by Epic Research, Inc., of Helena. Information in Figure 7 was compiled from listings supplied by Epic Research.

17. Author's correspondence with the North Dakota Highway Department, Bismarck, North Dakota, various dates, 1976–77.

18. William F. Lagrone and Earle E. Gavett, *Interstate Custom Combining in the Great Plains in 1971* (Washington, D.C.: Economic Research Service, 1975), passim. Information in Figure 8 derived from tables in this source.

CHAPTER 4

1. Fischer, "Custom Wheat Harvesting in the Economy of Western Oklahoma," pp. 89–90.

2. Ibid.

3. Information in Figure 9 was compiled from combine inspection registers of the Nebraska Bureau of Plant Industry, 1969.

4. Information in Figure 10 was compiled from the 1974 agricultural census. The census reported the total dollar value of custom work in each county, as well as the number of cultivated acres, making it possible to compute the dollar value of custom work per cultivated acre.

5. Percentages shown in Figure 11 were supplied by the Kansas Crop and Livestock Reporting Service, Topeka, Kansas.

6. Information in Table 4 was adapted from tables in *Uses of Agricultural Machinery in 1964*, Statistical Bulletin 377, Economic Research Service—Statistical Reporting Service, United States Department of Agriculture.

7. Lagrone and Gavett, *Interstate Custom Combining in the Great Plains in 1971*, p. 21.

8. This information derived from questionnaires returned to the author by custom combiners. Questionnaires were sent to nearly 200 custom cutters who bought permits in South Dakota in 1976. Forty were returned.

9. Comments enclosed with a questionnaire returned to the author.

10. John V. Hepler, *Farm Labor Program for Wheat and Small Grain Harvest in Great Plains States with Special Reference to Utilization of Migratory Workers in 1945* (Washington, D.C.: Agricultural Extension Service, 1946), p. 3.

11. Information on custom rates came from these sources: North Dakota State Employment Service, *North Dakota Harvest Labor Report*, 1948, 1949; North Dakota State Employment Service, *North Dakota Farm Labor Report*, 1950–53, including appended farm labor bulletins; H. K. Scott, *Farm Labor and Machinery Costs in Alberta, 1950* (Ottawa: Marketing Service, Dominion of Canada Department of Agriculture, 1952), p. 15; publications on custom rates by the Nebraska Crop and Livestock Reporting Service, 1957–59, 1962, 1968, 1970, excerpts provided by the Nebraska Crop and Livestock Reporting Service, Lincoln, Nebraska.

12. Information in Table 5 was extracted from these publications of the Kansas Crop and Livestock Reporting Service: *Custom Rates for Farm Operations*, 1961, 1965; *Rates for Custom Farm Operations*, 1970; *Kansas Custom Rates*, 1973, 1974, 1975, 1976. Additional information was from Ronald R. Poenisch and J. Michael Sprott, *Custom Farm Machinery Rates in Texas—1973*, Texas Agricultural Extension Service Fact Sheet L-1317; South Dakota Crop and Livestock Reporting Service, *Custom Rates for Farm Operations*, 1970, 1974; Saskatchewan Department of Agriculture, *1975 Custom Rates, 1976 Custom Rates*, and *1977 Custom Rates*.

13. Information about custom harvesting rates for milo came from the same sources as did information about custom rates for

wheat, especially the publications of the Kansas Crop and Livestock Reporting Service.

14. Kansas Crop and Livestock Reporting Service, *Rates for Custom Farm Operations*, 1970, and *Kansas Custom Rates*, 1976.

15. Quote from questionnaire returned to the author.

16. Fischer, "Custom Wheat Harvesting in the Economy of Western Oklahoma," pp. 14–15.

17. Hecht, *Transient Combine-Harvester-Thresher in the Great Plains, 1942*, appended map.

18. Lagrone and Gavett, *Interstate Custom Combining in the Great Plains in 1971*, p. 17.

19. Quotes from questionnaires returned to the author.

20. Ibid.

21. Personal interview with Loren Unruh, Great Bend, Kansas, January 9, 1977.

22. Personal interview with Ron Roessler, Buhler, Kansas, December 5, 1976.

23. Lagrone and Gavett, *Interstate Custom Combining in the Great Plains in 1971*, p. 16; questionnaires returned to the author.

CHAPTER 5

1. Comments enclosed with questionnaires returned to the author.

2. Ibid.

3. Fischer, "Custom Wheat Harvesting in the Economy of Western Oklahoma," pp. 30–31.

4. Averages were calculated from data in Lagrone and Gavett, *Interstate Custom Combining in the Great Plains in 1971*, p. 4.

5. Questionnaires returned to the author.

6. Hecht, *Transient Combine-Harvester-Threshers in the Great Plains, 1942*; Fischer, "Custom Wheat Harvesting in the Economy of Western Oklahoma," pp. 15–16.

7. Combine inspection registers, Nebraska Bureau of Plant Industry, 1969.

8. Lagrone and Gavett, *Interstate Custom Combining in the Great Plains in 1971*, p. 4.

9. Custom combiners' permits, Montana Department of Highways, 1976.

10. Combine inspection registers, Nebraska Bureau of Plant In-

dustry, 1969; Lagrone and Gavett, *Interstate Custom Combining in the Great Plains in 1971*, p. 5; custom combiners' permits, Montana Department of Highways, 1976.

11. Combine inspection registers, Nebraska Bureau of Plant Industry, 1969.

12. Averages computed from information on custom combiners' permits, Montana Department of Highways, 1976, and on South Dakota Non-Resident Custom Combiners Permits, South Dakota Department of Public Safety, 1976.

13. Lagrone and Gavett, *Interstate Custom Combining in the Great Plains in 1971*, p. 11; averages computed from information on custom combiners' permits, Montana Department of Highways, 1976, and on South Dakota Non-Resident Custom Combiners Permits, South Dakota Department of Public Safety, 1976.

14. Questionnaires returned to the author.

15. Lagrone and Gavett, *Interstate Custom Combining in the Great Plains in 1971*, pp. 3, 12–13.

16. Ibid., p. 11; questionnaires returned to the author.

17. Questionnaires returned to the author.

18. Personal interview with Melvin Jantz, Moundridge, Kansas, March 18, 1977.

19. Lagrone and Gavett, *Interstate Custom Combining in the Great Plains in 1971*, p. 22; custom combiners' permits, Montana Department of Highways, 1976.

20. Custom combiners' permits, Montana Department of Highways, 1976.

21. Personal interview with Elmer and Keith Dirks, Buhler, Kansas, December 28, 1976.

22. Combine inspection registers, Nebraska Bureau of Plant Industry, 1969; custom combiners' permits, Montana Department of Highways, 1976.

23. Allis-Chalmers Company and Massey-Ferguson, Inc., each year published brochures outlining the routes of their mobile parts units.

24. Hecht, *Transient Combine-Harvester-Threshers in the Great Plains*, 1942.

25. Lagrone and Gavett, *Interstate Custom Combining in the Great Plains in 1971*, p. 10; questionnaires returned to the author.

26. Personal interview with Henry Oldham.

27. Questionnaires returned to the author.

28. Personal interview with Ted Hardwick.

29. Hecht, *Transient Combine-Harvester-Threshers in the Great Plains, 1942*; combine inspection registers, Nebraska Bureau of Plant Industry, 1969.

30. Lagrone and Gavett, *Interstate Custom Combining in the Great Plains in 1971*, p. 20.

31. Ibid., p. 23.

32. Application and comments enclosed with a questionnaire returned to the author.

33. Questionnaires returned to the author.

34. Ibid.

35. Fischer, "Custom Wheat Harvesting in the Economy of Western Oklahoma," pp. 38–73, also appendix Table II.

36. William F. Lagrone and Charles C. Micheel, *Income and Expenses of Interstate Custom Combiners* (Washington, D.C.: Economic Research Service, 1975), pp. 5, 14–15.

37. Questionnaires returned to the author.

CHAPTER 6

1. Questionnaire returned to the author.

2. Hecht, *Transient Combine-Harvester-Threshers in the Great Plains, 1942*; Lagrone and Gavett, *Interstate Custom Combining in the Great Plains in 1971*, pp. 14–15.

3. Personal interview with Mable Squires.

4. Personal interview with Everett Squires.

5. Diaries of Flava Bever, Cedar Vale, Kansas.

6. Personal interviews with members of the crew of Bernel Elmore, near Vernon, Texas, during June, 1977.

7. Personal interviews with members of the crew of Richard Squires, near Taloga, Oklahoma, and Tribune, Kansas, during June, 1977; diaries of Flava Bever.

8. Personal interview with Jack Schlessiger.

9. *Newsweek*, Vol. 90, No. 1 (July 4, 1977), pp. 65–66.

10. Personal interview with Irvin and Margaret Zecha; Ann Montgomery, "'Wheaties' Share Problems Common to Small Town Life," *Foster County Independent* (Carrington, North Dakota), September 22, 1976, p. 25.

11. Personal interview with Ron Roessler.

12. Questionnaires returned to the author.

CHAPTER 7

1. Wayne D. Rasmussen, *A History of the Emergency Farm Labor Supply Program, 1943–47*, Agriculture Monograph 13, Bureau of Agricultural Economics, pp. 24, 34–45, 65–73, 90; War Food Administration, *Report of Cooperative Extension Work in Agriculture and Home Economics*, 1943, pp. 3–4.

2. Rasmussen, *History of the Emergency Farm Labor Supply Program, 1943–47*, pp. 78, 90; Leker, *Farm Labor Program for Wheat and Other Small Grain Harvest in the Great Plains States, 1943 to 1947*, p. 6.

3. Leker, *Farm Labor Program for Wheat and Other Small Grain Harvest in the Great Plains States, 1943 to 1947*, pp. 7–8.

4. "South Dakota Directs Itinerant Combines," *Extension Service Review*, Vol. 15, No. 2 (February, 1944), p. 19.

5. Leker, *Farm Labor Program for Wheat and Other Small Grain Harvest in the Great Plains States, 1943 to 1947*, pp. 8–9; Montana State Extension Service, *Custom Combine Operator's Guide for Montana*, 1944, p. 1.

6. Hepler, *Farm Labor Program for Wheat and Small Grain Harvest*, p. 1; Agricultural Extension Service, *Wheat and Small Grain Harvest, Western Great Plains States*, 1945, passim.

7. Leker, *Farm Labor Program for Wheat and Other Small Grain Harvest in the Great Plains States, 1943 to 1947*, pp. 9–10.

8. Hepler, *Farm Labor Program for Wheat and Small Grain Harvest*, pp. 6–9.

9. Ibid., pp. 9–11.

10. Ibid., pp. 12–17.

11. Ibid., pp. 16–18, 20.

12. Ibid., pp. 10–16; "Wheat Harvest Army Sweeps 10 States," *Extension Service Review*, Vol. 18, No. 7 (July, 1947), p. 87; Ralph W. Cessna, "The Combines Mobilize," *Christian Science Monitor Magazine Section*, August 17, 1946, p. 5; Agricultural Extension Service, *Combine and Labor Guide, Wheat and Small Grain Harvest*, United States Department of Agriculture Program Aid 29.

13. Gilkison, "Wheat Harvest Pattern," pp. 30–31; personal interview with Loyal Fortmeyer, Topeka, Kansas, September 2, 1976; personal interview with James Jay, Great Bend, Kansas, December 27, 1976.

14. Annual reports of the Farm Placement Service (Rural Man-

power Service) of the Oklahoma Employment Security Commission are variously titled as *Farm Labor Report* and *Rural Manpower Report* and were available for the years 1953, 1957–76. The above account also was based on a personal interview with John Shoemake, Oklahoma City, Oklahoma, April 8, 1977.

15. Annual reports of the Farm Placement Service (Rural Manpower Service) of the Nebraska State Employment Service, titled *Farm Labor Report* or *Rural Manpower Report*, 1948–76; personal interview with Don Christenson, Lincoln, Nebraska, January 12, 1977.

16. North Dakota State Employment Service, *North Dakota Harvest Labor Report*, for years 1948–1953; North Dakota Employment Security Bureau, *Rural Manpower Report*, 1975.

17. Author's correspondence with officials of the Job Service of South Dakota, the Montana State Employment Service, the Wyoming State Employment Service, and the Texas Employment Commission, various dates, 1976–77.

18. Farm Placement Service (United States Employment Service), *Wheat and Small Grain Harvest of the Great Plains States*, 1954.

19. Personal interview with Ted Hardwick.

20. Montana State Extension Service, *Custom Combine Operator's Guide for Montana*, 1944; "South Dakota Directs Itinerant Combines," p. 19.

21. Information about state statutes affecting custom cutters derived from correspondence with numerous state officials, from state guides for custom cutters bound into the annual reports of the farm placement services of the states, from the Agricultural Extension Service's *Wheat and Small Grain Harvest Map of the Great Plains States*, 1947, and from the Farm Placement Service's *Wheat and Small Grain Harvest of the Great Plains States*, 1954.

CHAPTER 8

1. "Organized Movements of Seasonal Workers in Agriculture," *Labour Gazette*, Vol. 49, No. 7 (July, 1949), pp. 834–39.

2. J. E. Snowball to M. E. Hartnett, June 18, 1946, numerous claims against the Saskatchewan Department of Agriculture asking compensation for transporting harvesting machinery, 1944–45, and list of claims paid in 1945, all in records of the Farm Labour Divi-

sion, Saskatchewan Department of Agriculture, Saskatchewan Archives Office, Regina, Saskatchewan.

3. "Co-operation Between Canada and United States in Harvesting of Crops," *Labour Gazette*, Vol. 47, No. 12 (December, 1947), pp. 1760–61; "United States and Canada Collaborate in Harvest Work," *Foreign Agriculture*, Vol. 6, No. 9 (September, 1942), pp. 340–41.

4. White House press release, April 10, 1942, copy supplied by the European-Canadian Desk, United States Department of State, Washington, D.C.

5. A. C. Devaney, memorandum, July 6, 1942, and D. F. Christy to Lemuel B. Schofield, July 7, 1942, both in File 56078/591, Immigration and Naturalization Service, United States Department of Justice, Washington, D.C.

6. T. M. Shoemaker, order of July 13, 1942, Lemuel B. Schofield to Cordell Hull, July 14, 1942, Adolf V. Berley to Francis Biddle, July 17, 1942, and "United States and Canadian Ports of Entry for Receiving Grain Harvesters and Machinery," undated, all in File 56078/591, Immigration and Naturalization Service.

7. Ibid., "To State Directors of the United States Employment Service in Montana, North Dakota, and Minnesota," undated.

8. Ibid., E. E. Adcock to the Commissioner of Immigration and Naturalization, September 18, 1942; W. W. Dawson to George V. Haythorne, January 7, 1943, and W. W. Dawson to Don Larin, September 24, 1942, both in records of the Farm Labour Division, Saskatchewan Department of Agriculture, Saskatchewan Archives Office.

9. D. W. Brewster to the Commissioner of Immigration and Naturalization, April 1, 1943, D. W. Brewster to the Commissioner of Immigration and Naturalization, April 12, 1943, and E. E. Adcock to the Commissioner of Immigration and Naturalization, April 28, 1943, all in File 56078/591, Immigration and Naturalization Service.

10. W. W. Dawson to Don Larin, September 24, 1942, and W. W. Dawson to George V. Haythorne, January 7, 1943, both in records of the Farm Labour Division, Saskatchewan Department of Agriculture, Saskatchewan Archives Office.

11. J. G. Parsons, memorandum of conversation, June 9, 1943, records of the Canadian Desk, Division of European Affairs, United States Department of State, File 811.504 Canada, National Archives and Records Service, Washington, D.C.; Administrator of the War

Food Administration to William Johnson, June 16, 1943, and William Johnson to Administrator of the War Food Administration, undated, both in records of the Office of Labor, War Food Administration, United States Department of Agriculture, Record Group 224, National Archives and Records Service, Washington, D.C.

12. A. W. Klieforth to the Secretary of State, August 19, 1943, Paul Armstrong to the Commissioner of Immigration and Naturalization, December 24, 1943, and D. W. Brewster to the Commissioner of Immigration and Naturalization, December 28, 1943, all in File 56079/591, Immigration and Naturalization Service.

13. War Food Administration, *Agreement for Movement of Grain Harvesting Labor and Machinery Between the United States and Canada*, 1943.

14. J. W. Willard to L. A. Wheeler, February 26, 1944, records of the Division of Foreign Agricultural Research, Office of Foreign Agricultural Relations, United States Department of Agriculture, Record Group 166, National Archives and Records Service, Washington, D.C.; Special Memorandum 90, undated, File 56078/591, Immigration and Naturalization Service.

15. National Selective Service Regional Circular R, June 21, 1944, records of the Farm Labour Division, Saskatchewan Department of Agriculture, Saskatchewan Archives Office, Regina, Saskatchewan; Jordan to Joseph Savoretti, February 20, 1945, File 56078/591, Immigration and Naturalization Service.

16. Joseph Savoretti, memorandum for Board of Immigration Appeals, May 18, 1945, Edward T. Wailes to Herbert H. Landon, May 5, 1945, and John Stewart to Robert H. Robinson (telephone conversation), May 26, 1945, all in File 56078/591, Immigration and Naturalization Service.

17. J. E. Snowball to M. E. Hartnett, June 18, 1946, records of the Farm Labour Division, Saskatchewan Department of Agriculture, Saskatchewan Archives Office.

18. Ibid., J. E. Snowball, list of custom combiners from Saskatchewan working in the United States, 1945.

19. Ray Atherton to the Secretary of State, August 24, 1945, File 56078/591, Immigration and Naturalization Service.

20. Ibid., L. A. Wheeler to Herbert H. Landon, undated, and Lewis Clark to the Secretary of State, April 18, 1946. George V. Haythorne, memorandum to H. R. Richardson, M. E. Hartnett, and R. M. Putnam, April 26, 1946, and Roy E. Fysh to Dominion-

Provincial Farm Labour Committee, November 12, 1947, both in records of the Farm Labour Division, Saskatchewan Department of Agriculture, Saskatchewan Archives Office; J. E. Snowball to M. E. Hartnett, October 17, 1946, and J. E. Snowball to M. E. Hartnett, October 28, 1946, both in records of the Dominion of Canada Department of Agriculture, Record Group 27, Vol. 3042, File 138, Public Archives of Canada, Ottawa, Ontario.

21. J. E. Snowball to M. E. Hartnett, October 17, 1946, records of the Dominion of Canada Department of Agriculture, Record Group 27, Vol. 3042, File 138, Public Archives of Canada.

22. Thomas W. Holland to Argyle Machey, May 16, 1947, and Ray Atherton to L. B. Pearson, May 19, 1947, both in File 56078/591, Immigration and Naturalization Service; "Report of Conference with U.S. and State Officials on Harvest Labour Held at Dodge City and Hays, Kansas, on April 29 and 30, 1947," records of the Farm Labour Division, Saskatchewan Department of Agriculture, Saskatchewan Archives Office.

23. G. J. McGee to H. R. Richardson, R. M. Putnam, and E. E. Brockelbank, April 24, 1947, and Roy E. Fysh to the Dominion-Provincial Farm Labour Committee, undated, both in records of the Farm Labour Division, Saskatchewan Department of Agriculture, Saskatchewan Archives Office.

24. Bernard Joy to M. L. Wilson, July 2, 1947, attachment to Leker, *Farm Labor Program for Wheat and Other Small Grain Harvest in the Great Plains States, 1943 to 1947.*

25. Roy E. Fysh to the Dominion-Provincial Farm Labour Committee, November 12, 1947, and E. E. Brockelbank to R. M. Putnam, January 27, 1948, both in records of the Farm Labour Division, Saskatchewan Department of Agriculture, Saskatchewan Archives Office.

26. J. R. Bunn to J. B. Kidd, May 22, 1947, unheaded memorandum, June 6, 1947, and memorandum to the District Director of the Immigration and Naturalization Service in San Antonio, June 18, 1947, all in File 56078/591, Immigration and Naturalization Service.

27. Ibid., R. H. Robinson, memorandum, July 2, 1948, and A. W. Motley to Willard F. Kelly, July 28, 1949.

28. Letters exchanged for the years 1948–52 are in records of the Dominion of Canada Department of Agriculture, Record Group 17, Vol. 3130, File 66–5–1, Public Archives of Canada, Ottawa, Ontario.

29. Lagrone and Gavett, *Custom Combining in the Great Plains in 1971*, pp. 2–3.

CHAPTER 9

1. All information about the Irvin Zecha outfit in this chapter came from interviews with Irvin Zecha and Margaret Zecha or from daily logbooks that Zecha kept on the harvest. The author interviewed the Zechas on January 9, 1977, and on January 5, 1978. During harvest Zecha usually maintained a daily logbook with a record of hours worked by his hired men, and most of these logbooks are in his possession.

2. The going rate shown in Table 10 was determined from lists of customers and revenues in Zecha's logbooks. In all cases it was clear from the figures that a single rate predominated, and that variations from it usually were designed to fit special conditions.

3. Information in Table 11 derived from lists of customers in Zecha's logbooks.

4. Ibid.

5. Information about hours and wages of hired men appeared in the back of most of the logbooks.

6. The years 1955, 1962, and 1971 were selected because they were distributed well through the years of Zecha's career and because complete logbooks were available for those years. A "Cutting Day" as shown in the table was one during which the outfit harvested for four hours or more; a "Partial Cutting Day" was one during which the outfit harvested for less than four hours; an "Idle Day" was one during which the outfit did not harvest or travel at all.

7. Walter P. Webb, *The Great Plains* (Boston: Ginn and Co., 1931).

8. James C. Malin, *Winter Wheat in the Golden Belt of Kansas: A Study in Adaptation to Subhumid Geographical Environment.* Reprint. (New York: Octagon Books, 1973); Leslie Hewes, *The Suitcase Farming Frontier: A Study in the Historical Geography of the Central Great Plains* (Lincoln: University of Nebraska Press, 1973).

9. Carl F. Kraenzel, *The Great Plains in Transition* (Norman: University of Oklahoma Press, 1955).

Bibliography

PUBLISHED WORKS

Agricultural Extension Service, United States Department of Agriculture. *Combine and Labor Guide, Wheat and Small Grain Harvest*. United States Department of Agriculture Program Aid 29. 1947.

————. *Wheat and Small Grain Harvest Map of the Great Plains States*. 1947.

————. *Wheat and Small Grain Harvest, Western Great Plains States*. 1945.

Aicher, L. C. "Problems of the Combine Harvester." *Report of the Kansas State Board of Agriculture for the Quarter Ending March, 1930*.

Allen, Henry J. "The New Harvest Hand." *American Review of Reviews*, Vol. 76, No. 3 (September, 1927), pp. 279–84.

The American Press Salutes the Harvest Brigade. Toronto: Massey-Harris Co., n.d. Publicity brochure. Copy in library of Massey-Ferguson Co., Toronto, Ontario.

Arnold, J. H. "Farm Practices in Growing Wheat." *Yearbook of the United States Department of Agriculture, 1919*. Washington, D.C.: Government Printing Office, 1920.

Benedict, Murray R. *Farm Policies of the United States, 1790–1950: A Study of Their Origins and Development*. New York: Twentieth Century Fund, 1953.

Benton, Alva H., R. H. Black, W. R. Humphries, W. M. Hurst, C. E. Mangels, R. C. Miller, L. A. Reynoldson, H. E. Shielstad, and T. E. Stoa. *The Combined Harvester-Thresher in North Dakota*. North Dakota Agricultural Experiment Station Bulletin 225. 1929.

Bureau of the Census. *Manufacture and Sale of Farm Equipment and Related Products, 1942.* Washington, D.C.: Government Printing Office, 1943.

———. *Production and Sales of Farm Machines and Equipment, 1944.* Washington, D.C.: Government Printing Office, 1945.

Carhart, Arthur H. "Hammtown—U. S. A." *Rotarian,* Vol. 15, No. 1 (July, 1949), pp. 17–20.

Carroll, Tom. "Basic Requirements in the Design and Development of the Self-propelled Combine." *Agricultural Engineering,* Vol. 29, No. 3 (March, 1948), pp. 101–3.

Cessna, Ralph W. "The Combines Mobilize." *Christian Science Monitor Magazine,* August 17, 1946, p. 5.

Church, Lillian. *Partial History of the Development of Grain Threshing Implements.* Information Series 73, Bureau of Agricultural Engineering, United States Department of Agriculture. 1939.

"Combines Follow Harvest." *Capper's Farmer,* Vol. 55, No. 5 (May, 1944), p. 23.

"Co-operation Between Canada and United States in Harvesting of Crops." *Labour Gazette,* Vol. 47, No. 12 (December, 1947), pp. 1760–64.

Cullum, Robert M., Josiah C. Folsom, and Donald G. Hay. *Men and Machines in the North Dakota Harvest.* Washington, D.C.: Bureau of Agricultural Economics, 1942.

———. *Men and Machines in the North Dakota Harvest (Statistical Supplement).* Washington, D.C.: Bureau of Agricultural Economics, 1942.

Currier, E. L. *The Cost of Growing Wheat in Typical Non-irrigated Areas in Montana.* Montana Agricultural Experiment Station Bulletin 122. 1918.

Denison, Merrill. *Harvest Triumphant: The Story of Massey-Harris.* New York: Dodd, Mead, and Co., 1949.

Drache, Hiram M. *Beyond the Furrow: Some Keys to Successful Farming in the Twentieth Century.* Danville, Illinois: Interstate Printers and Publishers, 1976.

———. *The Day of the Bonanza: Bonanza Farming in the Red River Valley of the North.* Fargo: North Dakota Institute for Regional Studies, 1964.

Ellsworth, J. O. and R. W. Baird. *The Combine Harvester on Oklahoma Farms, 1926.* Oklahoma Agricultural Experiment Station Bulletin 162. 1927.

"An Extra Million Acre Harvest." *Farm Implement News*, March 30, 1944, pp. 26–27.

"Farm Equipment Available in 1944." *Agricultural Situation*, Vol. 27, No. 2 (February, 1944), pp. 15–16.

"Farm Machinery in Wartime." *Agricultural Situation*, Vol. 29, No. 6 (June, 1945), pp. 14–17.

Farm Placement Service, United States Employment Service. *Wheat and Small Grain Harvest of the Great Plains States.* 1954.

Fite, Gilbert C. *The Farmers' Frontier, 1865–1900.* New York: Holt, Rinehart, and Winston, 1966. Reprint. Albuquerque: University of New Mexico Press, 1977.

"Flying Harvest Hand." *Business Week*, No. 775 (July 8, 1944), p. 48.

Gilkison, Robert B. "Wheat Harvest Pattern." *Employment Security Review*, Vol. 27, No. 3 (March, 1950), pp. 30–31.

Grimes, W. E. "The Effect of the Combined Harvester-Thresher on Farming in a Wheat Growing Region." *Scientific Agriculture*, Vol. 9, No. 12 (August, 1929), pp. 773–82.

Grimes, W. E., R. S. Kifer, and J. A. Hodges. *The Effect of the Combined Harvester-Thresher on Farm Organization in Southwestern Kansas and Northwestern Oklahoma.* Kansas Agricultural Experiment Station Circular 142. 1929.

"Gypsies of the Harvest." *Newsweek*, Vol. 90, No. 1 (July 4, 1977), pp. 65–66.

Hardy, Evan A. "The Combine Harvester in Western Canada." *Scientific Agriculture*, Vol. 12, No. 3 (November, 1931), pp. 121–29.

———. "The Combine in Canada." *American Thresherman*, May, 1931, pp. 9, 17.

———. "The 'Combine' in Saskatchewan." *Agricultural Situation*, Vol. 8, No. 8 (August, 1927), pp. 206–8.

———. "The Combine in the Prairie Provinces." *Agricultural Engineering*, Vol. 10, No. 2 (February, 1929), pp. 55–56.

———. "Combines, Old and New." *Nor'West Farmer*, May 21, 1928, pp. 7, 12–13, 15.

"Harvest Brigade." *Time*, Vol. 44, No. 5 (July 31, 1944), p. 79.

"Harvesting Corn by Combine," a symposium of papers. *Agricultural Engineering*, Vol. 36, No. 12 (December, 1955), pp. 791–802.

"Harvesting Race: Massey-Harris Spots Its Self-propelled Combines in Areas of Acute Machine Shortage, Offers Prizes for Best

Performance." *Business Week*, No. 764 (April 22, 1944), pp. 26, 29.

Haystead, Ladd and Gilbert C. Fite. *The Agricultural Regions of the United States*. Norman: University of Oklahoma Press, 1955.

The Header Barge Method of Harvesting. Alberta Agricultural Extension Circular 14. n.d.

Hecht, Reuben W. *Transient Combine-Harvester-Threshers in the Great Plains, 1942*. Washington, D.C.: Bureau of Agricultural Economics, 1942. Copy in File 56078/591, Immigration and Naturalization Service, United States Department of Justice, Washington, D.C.

Hepler, John V. *Farm Labor Program for Wheat and Small Grain Harvest in Great Plains States with Special Reference to Utilization of Migratory Workers in 1945*. Washington, D.C.: Agricultural Extension Service, United States Department of Agriculture, 1946.

Hewes, Leslie. *The Suitcase Farming Frontier: A Study in the Historical Geography of the Central Great Plains*. Lincoln: University of Nebraska Press, 1973.

Higgins, F. Hal. "The Cradle of the Combine." *Pacific Rural Press*, Vol. 133, No. 8 (February 20, 1937), pp. 284–85.

———. "John M. Horner and the Development of the Combined Harvester." *Agricultural History*, Vol. 32, No. 1 (January, 1958), pp. 14–24.

———. "The Moore-Hascall Harvester Centennial Approaches." *Michigan History*, Vol. 14, No. 3 (July, 1930), pp. 415–37.

"Homeless Wheat." *Business Week*, No. 660 (April 25, 1942), pp. 81–82.

Hunger, Edwin A. "Kansas Outstanding Leader in the Use of the Combine." *Twenty-seventh Biennial Report of the Kansas State Board of Agriculture*. 1930.

Johannsen, W. S. "The Great Migration." *Implement and Tractor*, July 31, 1943, pp. 10–12, 23.

Kansas Crop and Livestock Reporting Service. Reports on custom rates, titles vary. 1961, 1965, 1970, 1973, 1976.

Kay, Ronald D., Kenneth R. Poenisch, and J. Michael Sprott. *Custom Farm Machinery Rates in Texas—1973*. Texas Agricultural Extension Service Fact Sheet L-1317. 1974.

Kraenzel, Carl F. *The Great Plains in Transition*. Norman: University of Oklahoma Press, 1955.

Lagrone, William F. and Charles C. Micheel. *Income and Expenses of Interstate Custom Combiners*. Washington, D.C.: Economic Research Service, United States Department of Agriculture, 1975.

Lagrone, William F. and Earle E. Gavett. *Interstate Custom Combining in the Great Plains in 1971*. Washington, D.C.: Economic Research Service, United States Department of Agriculture, 1975.

Leker, E. H. *Farm Labor Program for Wheat and Other Small Grain Harvest in the Great Plains States, 1943 to 1947*. Washington, D.C.: Agricultural Extension Service, 1948.

Lescohier, Don D. *Conditions Affecting the Demand for Harvest Labor in the Wheat Belt*. United States Department of Agriculture Bulletin 1230. 1924.

———. *Harvest Labor Problems in the Wheat Belt*. United States Department of Agriculture Bulletin 1020. 1922.

———. *Sources of Supply and Conditions of Employment of Harvest Labor in the Wheat Belt*. United States Department of Agriculture Bulletin 1211. 1924.

Lundy, Gabriel. *The Header Stack-Barge for Harvesting*. Special Extension Circular 7, South Dakota Extension Service. 1930.

Lundy, Gabriel, L. H. Klages, and J. F. Goss. *The Use of the Combine in South Dakota*. South Dakota Agricultural Experiment Station Bulletin 244. 1930.

McColly, H. F. "The Combine in the Spring Wheat Area." *American Thresherman*, May, 1931, pp. 8–9.

Mackenzie, J. K. "The Windrow Harvester." *American Thresherman*, May, 1931, pp. 5, 18.

Malin, James C. *Winter Wheat in the Golden Belt of Kansas: A Study in Adaptation to Subhumid Geographic Environment*. Reprint. New York: Octagon Books, 1973.

"Massey-Harris Forms Self-propelled Combine Brigade to Harvest 1944 Crops." *Implement Record*, April, 1944. Copy in clippings collections, John Deere Co. Archives, Moline, Illinois.

Massey-Harris Self-propelled Harvest Brigade. Toronto: Massey-Harris Co., n.d. Publicity brochure. Copy in library of Massey-Ferguson Co., Toronto, Ontario.

Mayer, I. D. "Windrow and Pick-up Attachments." *Agricultural Engineering*, Vol. 10, No. 2 (February, 1929), pp. 67–68.

Miller, Merritt Finley. *The Evolution of Reaping Machines*. Office of Experiment Stations Bulletin 103, United States Department of Agriculture. 1902.

Miller, R. C. "The Combine in North Dakota." *Agricultural Engineering*, Vol. 7, No. 5 (May, 1927), pp. 115–16.

Montana State Employment Service. Annual farm labor reports, titles vary. 1956–58, 1962–64, 1967–70, 1974–76.

Montana State Extension Service. *Custom Combine Operator's Guide for Montana.* 1944.

Montgomery, Ann. "'Wheaties' Share Problems Common to Small Town Life." *Foster County Independent* (Carrington, North Dakota), September 22, 1976, p. 25.

Mullen, C. W. "Custom Combines." *Power Farming*, Vol. 37, No. 4 (April, 1928), p. 8.

Nebraska Crop and Livestock Reporting Service. Annual reports on custom rates, titles vary. 1957–59, 1962, 1964, 1966, 1968, 1970, 1972, 1974.

Nebraska State Employment Service. Annual farm labor reports, titles vary. 1948–75. Copies in files of the Nebraska Department of Labor, Lincoln, Nebraska.

North Dakota State Employment Service. Annual farm labor reports, titles vary. 1948–53.

Oklahoma Employment Security Commission. Annual farm labor reports, titles vary. 1953, 1957–76.

"Operating a 95,000-Acre Wheat Farm." *Mechanical Engineering*, Vol. 50, No. 10 (October, 1928), pp. 748–52.

"Organized Movements of Seasonal Workers in Agriculture." *Labour Gazette*, Vol. 49, No. 7 (July, 1949), pp. 834–41.

Ottoson, Howard W., Eleanor M. Birch, Philip A. Henderson, and A. H. Anderson. *Land and People in the Northern Plains Transition Area.* Lincoln: University of Nebraska Press, 1966.

Pickard, George E. *Combining, Drying, and Storing of Corn.* Moline: John Deere Co., n.d. Technical brochure, copy in John Deere Co. Archives.

Preliminary Survey of Major Areas Requiring Outside Agricultural Labor. Extension Farm Labor Circular 38, Agricultural Extension Service, United States Department of Agriculture.

Rasmussen, Wayne D. *A History of the Emergency Farm Labor Supply Program, 1943–47.* Agriculture Monograph 13, Bureau of Agricultural Economics, United States Department of Agriculture, 1951.

Reynoldson, L. A., R. S. Kifer, J. H. Martin, and W. R. Humphries. *The Combined Harvester-Thresher in the Great Plains.* United States Department of Agriculture Technical Bulletin 70. 1928.

"Rotary 'Shock Troops' to the Rescue." *Rotarian*, Vol. 41, No. 4 (October, 1942), pp. 23–24.

Rundles, J. C. "The Thrashing Ring in the Corn Belt." *Yearbook of the United States Department of Agriculture, 1918.* Washington, D.C.: Government Printing Office, 1919.

Saskatchewan Department of Agriculture. *Custom Rates.* 1975–77.

Schlebeker, John T. *Whereby We Thrive: A History of American Farming, 1607–1972.* Ames: Iowa State University Press, 1975.

Schob, David E. *Hired Hands and Plowboys: Farm Labor in the Midwest, 1815–60.* Urbana: University of Illinois Press, 1975.

Schwantes, A. J. "Windrow Method of Combine Harvesting." *Agricultural Engineering*, Vol. 10, No. 2 (February, 1929), pp. 49–50.

Scott, H. K. *Farm Labor and Machinery Costs in Alberta, 1950.* Ottawa: Marketing Service, Dominion of Canada Department of Agriculture, 1952.

Smith, H. P. and Robert P. Spilman. *Harvesting Grain with the Combined Harvester-Thresher in Northwest Texas.* Texas Agricultural Experiment Station Bulletin 373. 1927.

"South Dakota Directs Itinerant Combines." *Extension Service Review*, Vol. 15, No. 2 (February, 1944), p. 19.

Starch, A. E. and R. M. Merrill. *The Combined Harvester-Thresher in Montana.* Montana Agricultural Experiment Station Bulletin 230. 1930.

Streeter, C. P. "Here Come the Combines." *Farm Journal*, Vol. 71, No. 8 (August, 1947), pp. 20–21.

Taggart, J. G. and J. K. Mackenzie. *Seven Years' Experience with the Combined Reaper-Thresher.* Dominion of Canada Department of Agriculture Bulletin 118. 1929.

Taylor, Paul S. "Migratory Laborers in the Wheat Belt: Second Half of Nineteenth Century." Typescript produced by the University of California at Davis, 1957.

Thomas, Lewis H. "Early Combines in Saskatchewan." *Saskatchewan History*, Vol. 8, No. 1 (Winter, 1955), pp. 1–5.

Tucker, Joe. "The Self-propelled Combine." *Agricultural Engineering*, Vol. 25, No. 9 (September, 1944), pp. 333–35.

"United States and Canada Collaborate in Harvest Work." *Foreign*

Agriculture, Vol. 6, No. 9 (September, 1942), pp. 340–41.
Uses of Agricultural Machinery in 1964. Statistical Bulletin 377, Economic Research Service—Statistical Reporting Service, United States Department of Agriculture. 1965.
Walker, H. B. and E. L. Rhodes. "The Combine Harvester in Kansas." *Wheat in Kansas: Report of the Kansas State Board of Agriculture* for the Quarter Ending September, 1920.
War Food Administration, United States Department of Agriculture. *Agreement for Movement of Grain Harvesting Labor and Machinery Between the United States and Canada*. 1943.
————. *Report of Cooperative Extension Work in Agriculture and Home Economics*. 1943.
"We Did It Before." *Country Gentleman*, Vol. 113, No. 5 (May, 1943), pp. 20, 64.
Webb, Walter P. *The Great Plains*. Boston: Ginn and Co., 1931.
"West." *Agricultural Situation*, Vol. 27, No. 10 (October, 1943), pp. 18–19.
"Wheat Bonanza." *Business Week*, No. 615 (June 14, 1941), pp. 70–72.
"Wheat Harvest Army Sweeps 10 States." *Extension Service Review*, Vol. 18, No. 7 (July, 1947), p. 87.
"Wheat Outlook." *Agricultural Situation*, Vol. 27, No. 7 (July, 1943), pp. 14–15.
Wiant, D. E. and R. L. Patty. *Combining Grain in Weed-free Fields*. South Dakota Agricultural Experiment Station Bulletin 251. 1930.
Wickard, Claude R. "Wheat Farming in Wartime." *Vital Speeches of the Day*, Vol. 8, No. 15 (May 15, 1942), pp. 474–77.
Wilcox, Walter W. *The Farmer in the Second World War*. Ames: Iowa State College Press, 1947.
Williams, Charles M. "Enterprise on the Prairies." *Harvard Business Review*, Vol. 31, No. 2 (March-April, 1953), pp. 97–102.
Yerkes, Arnold P., and L. M. Church. *Cost of Harvesting Wheat by Different Methods*. United States Department of Agriculture Bulletin 627. 1918.

UNPUBLISHED SOURCES

Acker, Archie. "Memoirs of L. A. Pierce." Typescript of interview, August 3, 1936, Panhandle-Plains Historical Museum, Canyon, Texas.

Bever, Flava. Diaries, 1952–59. In her possession, Cedar Vale, Kansas.

Clippings collections. John Deere Co. Archives, Moline, Illinois.

Clippings collections. Kansas State Historical Society Library, Topeka, Kansas.

Division of Motor Vehicles, South Dakota Department of Public Safety, Pierre, South Dakota. South Dakota Non-Resident Custom Combiners Permits, 1976.

"Early Combines in Saskatchewan." Typescript of clippings, Saskatchewan Archives Office, Regina, Saskatchewan.

Fischer, John Lewis. "Custom Wheat Harvesting in the Economy of Western Oklahoma." Master of Science thesis, Oklahoma Agricultural and Mechanical College, 1949.

Harper, George D. "Eighty Years of Recollections." Typescript, Panhandle-Plains Historical Museum, Canyon, Texas.

Immigration and Naturalization Service, United States Department of Justice, Washington, D.C. File 56078/591.

Montana Department of Highways, Helena, Montana. Permits issued to custom combiners in Montana, 1976. Compiled into a report by Epic Research, Helena.

Noxious Weeds Division, Bureau of Plant Industry, Nebraska State Department of Agriculture, Lincoln, Nebraska. Registers of custom combines inspected at ports of entry, 1969. Destroyed when the Department of Agriculture moved its offices in 1977; only copies extant are photocopies in possession of the author.

Records of the Canadian Desk, Division of European Affairs, United States Department of State, File 811.504 Canada. National Archives and Records Service, Washington, D.C.

Records of the Division of Foreign Agricultural Research, Office of Foreign Agricultural Relations, United States Department of Agriculture. Record Group 166, National Archives and Records Service, Washington, D.C.

Records of the Dominion of Canada Department of Agriculture. Record Group 17, Vol. 3130, File 66–5–1, Public Archives of Canada, Ottawa, Ontario.

Records of the Dominion of Canada Department of Agriculture. Record Group 27, Vol. 3042, File 138, Public Archives of Canada, Ottawa, Ontario.

Records of the Farm Labour Division, Saskatchewan Department of Agriculture. Saskatchewan Archives Office, Regina, Saskatchewan.

Records of the Office of Labor, War Food Administration, United States Department of Agriculture. Record Group 224, National Archives and Records Service, Washington, D.C.

Redpath, F. M. "Cradle to Combine." Typescript, Kansas State Historical Society Library, Topeka, Kansas.

Summers, Sadie. "Memoirs of John Bell Porter." Typescript of interview, August 4, 1936, Panhandle-Plains Historical Museum, Canyon, Texas.

Zecha, Irvin. Daily logbooks, 1955–62, 1964–71. In his possession, Great Bend, Kansas.

PERSONAL INTERVIEWS BY THE AUTHOR

Bakken, Mervin and Ione Bakken, Homestead, Montana. Custom combiners. Interviewed at Taloga, Oklahoma, June 13, 1977.

Bever, Floyd, Sedan, Kansas. Former thresherman. Interviewed at Sedan, Kansas, April 13, 1976.

Christenson, Don, Lincoln, Nebraska. Director of the Nebraska Rural Manpower Service. Interviewed in Lincoln, Nebraska, January 12, 1977.

Cobb, Wheeler, Blackwell, Oklahoma. Mechanic and former custom combiner. Interviewed at Blackwell, Oklahoma, December 15, 1976.

Davis, Charles, Nardin, Oklahoma. Custom combiner. Interviewed at Blackwell, Oklahoma, December 15, 1976.

Dirks, Elmer, and Keith Dirks, Buhler, Kansas. Custom combiners. Interviewed at Buhler, Kansas, December 28, 1976.

Elmore, Bernel, and Neva Elmore, Shattuck, Oklahoma. Custom combiners. First interviewed at Vernon, Texas, June 8–10, 1977, and again at Watkins, Colorado, July 17–18, 1978. Additional interviews with Gary Elmore and with most members of the Elmore crew.

Fortmeyer, Loyal, Topeka, Kansas. Director of the Kansas Rural Manpower Service. Interviewed at Topeka, Kansas, September 2, 1976.

Gaines, Joe and Mary Beth Gaines, Peabody, Kansas. Custom combiners. Interviewed at Peabody, Kansas, March 18, 1977.

Habiger, Joe, Bushton, Kansas. Implement dealer. Interviewed at Bushton, Kansas, March 15, 1977.

Hachmeister, Cindy, Hays, Kansas. Truck driver. Interviewed at Taloga, Oklahoma, June 11, 1977.

Hardwick, Ted, Saxmon, Kansas. Custom combiner. Interviewed at Saxmon, Kansas, March 16, 1977.

Hildebrand, Charles and Dave Hildebrand, Vici, Oklahoma. Custom combiners. Interviewed at Vici, Oklahoma, March 7, 1977.

Howe, Clair, Chet Howe, and Donna Howe, Torrington, Wyoming. Custom combiners. First interviewed at Taloga, Oklahoma, June 11–12, 1977, and again at Torrington, Wyoming, July 12–13, 1978. Additional interviews with all members of the Howe crew.

Jantz, Melvin, Moundridge, Kansas. Partner in Jantz Manufacturing Co. Interviewed at Moundridge, Kansas, March 18, 1977.

Jay, James, Great Bend, Kansas. Former director of the Harvest Control Office. Interviewed at Great Bend, Kansas, December 27, 1976.

Johnson, Ernest, Vici, Oklahoma. Custom combiner. Interviewed at Vici, Oklahoma, April 6, 1977.

Keast, Taryn, Hutchinson, Kansas. Truck driver. Interviewed at Taloga, Oklahoma, June 11, 1977.

Oldham, Henry, Blackwell, Oklahoma. Implement dealer. Interviewed at Blackwell, Oklahoma, December 15, 1976.

Quig, Levi, Great Bend, Kansas. Custom combiner. Interviewed at Great Bend, Kansas, March 16, 1977.

Ring, W. H., Sedgwick, Kansas. Custom combiner. Interviewed at Stillwater, Oklahoma, October 14, 1978.

Roessler, Ron, Buhler, Kansas. Custom combiner. Interviewed at Buhler, Kansas, December 5, 1976.

Schlessiger, Jack and Jan Schlessiger, Claflin, Kansas. Custom combiners. Interviewed at Claflin, Kansas, March 17, 1977.

Shoemake, John, Oklahoma City, Oklahoma. Director of the Oklahoma Rural Manpower Service. Interviewed at Oklahoma City, Oklahoma, April 8, 1977.

Snell, Russell, Ellinwood, Kansas. Custom combiner. Interviewed at Ellinwood, Kansas, March 13, 1977.

Squires, Everett and Mable Squires, Taloga, Oklahoma. Custom combiners. Interviewed at Taloga, Oklahoma, June 10–11, 13, 1977.

Squires, Richard and Lois Squires, Taloga, Oklahoma. Custom combiners. First interviewed at Taloga, Oklahoma, June 10–11, 1977, and again at Tribune, Kansas, July 1–2, 1977.

Unruh, Loren, Great Bend, Kansas. Custom combiner and restaurant owner. Interviewed at Great Bend, Kansas, January 9, 1977.

Vater, Joe, Enid, Oklahoma. Implement dealer. Interviewed at Enid, Oklahoma, December 15, 1976.

White, Ruben, Brownwood, Texas. Custom combiner. Interviewed at Taloga, Oklahoma, June 10–11, 1977. Additional interviews with members of the White crew.

Zecha, Irvin and Margaret Zecha, Great Bend, Kansas. Custom combiners. First interviewed at Great Bend, Kansas, January 9, 1977, and again at Great Bend, January 5, 1978.

Index